Take the Name of Jesus with You

Take the Name of Jesus with You

A Practical Guide for Reaching Your Community through Prayer

Judy Garlow Wade

Judy Garlow Wade 6/03

wesleyan
publishing
house

Indianapolis, Indiana

To my children—

Son, Cade
Daughters, Cassandra and Christina
You have taught me to pray, for which I am grateful.

Contents

Preface

Several years ago, I heard someone say the word *prayerwalking*, and I grasped the idea immediately. I got so excited about it that I began to prayerwalk right away and asked some friends to join me. Prayerwalking filled us with both a longing to discover God's heart for our city and the hope that our community could be changed through prayer. It increased our desire for the Word, which in turn increased our faith and boldness.

About six months later, Steve Hawthorne, who had written a book on prayerwalking, spoke on this subject at our church. We were relieved to discover that we had instinctively done many of the right things. Steve was the first of many seasoned prayerwalkers who helped us refine our methods. We also learned much by trial and error. This is the journey that I share with you. Each chapter of this book contains the story of one of our prayerwalking experiences. You'll see the places we visited, the challenges we faced, the victories—and some failures. Each experience illustrates one aspect of prayerwalking, which is described more fully in the rest of the chapter.

This is not a textbook, however. It's more like a manual for beginning prayerwalkers. In every chapter, you'll find two resources that will enable you to begin prayerwalking right away, today, if you wish. First is the Prayer Action List, a simple checklist of things to do before, during, or after your prayerwalk. Each list targets a particular aspect of prayerwalking. Use these checklists until you gain more confidence at prayerwalking.

Second, each chapter includes a Prayer Focus Sheet. The Prayer Focus Sheet is an agenda for prayer, based on a specific location, issue, or aspect of prayer. The idea is simple: use these selected Scriptures and thoughts for prayer to help you get started and maintain your focus as you prayerwalk. I often use these or similar prayer focus sheets while praying for my community. You could actually use this book while you prayerwalk.

I pray that God will bless you and multiply your desire to reach your community through prayer. May you be empowered, emboldened, and filled with His Spirit as you take the name of Jesus with you wherever you go.

JUDY GARLOW WADE

Acknowledgements

I want to express my appreciation to my husband, Keat, who is a prayer partner and constant source of support; to Dionne Carpenter, who helped me with the manuscript; to Jody Wood, for valuable advice; to Pam Faraone, for reading the manuscript; to Suzanne Burgess and Glenda Pettit, who are such encouraging, faithful friends and intercessors; to all the prayerwalkers who have walked with me; to my mother, Winifred Garlow, who faithfully proofread every word many times; to my father, Burtis Garlow, (who would have loved the title) now deceased, for a lifetime of inspiration and example; to my brother, Jim Garlow, my biggest cheerleader for this book; and to my editor, Lawrence Wilson, with whom it was a joy to work.

My Presence will go with you. . . .
—Exodus 33:14

Every place that the sole of your foot will tread upon I have given you. . . .
—Joshua 1:3

Jehovah Shammah

The Lord Is There

This book is designed for people who want to pray more intelligently for their communities. It introduces the concept of *prayerwalking* and provides basic tools for either beginning or becoming more effective at this simple approach to prayer. God will give you the blueprint for praying for your own community; this book will give you a place to start.

I like to think of prayerwalking as a mobile prayer meeting—where God supplies the audiovisuals! A more standard definition of prayerwalking was written by Steve Hawthorne, author of *Prayerwalking: Praying On site with Insight.* Steve says that prayerwalking is "walking while praying and praying in the places where you expect your prayers to be answered."[1]

Pastor and author Ted Haggard defines prayerwalking as "walking through an area while interceding for that place" with the aim of improving our communities. He goes on to point out the benefits of walking while praying. "Praying while walking makes prayer purposeful, informed and stimulating. Moving about keeps your mind from wandering." Haggard continues, "If we are faithful to the Lord and willing to call on His name for our land, we will be victorious in hindering negative spiritual activity—the type of activity that promotes alcoholism, sexual sin, resentfulness, bitterness, and rebellion."[2]

As God's people, we have been given the awesome privilege and responsibility of interceding for our world. As we prayerwalk, we can change the world for the better.

The idea of prayerwalking is really nothing new. It has a solid precedent in Scripture. Deuteronomy 11:22–25 reads:

> If you carefully observe all these commands I am giving you to follow—to love the LORD your God, to walk in all His ways and to hold fast to Him—then the LORD will drive out all these nations before you and you will dispossess nations larger and stronger than you. *Every place where you set your foot will be yours.* . . . No man will be able to stand against you. The LORD your God, as he promised you, will put the terror and fear of you on the whole land, wherever you go (NIV, emphasis added).

Common Questions about Prayerwalking

I've noticed that beginning prayerwalkers often ask similar questions. There are initial hurdles they must clear before they feel comfortable trying this kind of ministry. Some wonder if they really are intercessors. Others are intimidated by the idea of praying in a small group of believers, let alone in a public place. A few wonder if they "have what it takes" spiritually to confront the problems in their community head-on, or if they'll know what to do when they prayerwalk.

I believe that every Christian can be a prayerwalker, regardless of his or her primary spiritual gifts. This is something you *can* do. Having answers to some basic questions about prayerwalking may give you the confidence to begin.

Am I an Intercessor?

While God commands all Christians to pray regularly, some believers seem especially gifted at praying effectively. These are called *intercessors*. To intercede is simply to plead on behalf of another. I like my husband's definition of intercession. Keat says, "For the intercessor, intercession is a condition of the heart. Prayer is a first response."

While some people are especially gifted to pray effectively, all Christians can and should pray. So this book is for you, whether you consider yourself to be an intercessor or not. When you prayerwalk, you will do the task of intercession, and God will bless your efforts. Your prayers will add weight to those of many fine believers who have prayed over the same territory, perhaps for many years. One day, God will give a breakthrough.

Is Prayerwalking Intimidating?

I've found that prayerwalking is best done somewhat anonymously. Generally, I don't want anyone to know that I am praying when I prayerwalk in public places. This is not because I'm afraid or trying to hide something, but because I want perfect freedom to listen to the Father, do what I need to do, and walk where I need to walk. I aim to look nonchalant, casual. Often I take along a camera or similar prop that provides a logical explanation for strolling or standing in an area. Anonymity provides greater freedom. Also, if I inadvertently do something that calls attention to myself, God will not be dishonored.

It's a good idea to prayerwalk with more experienced intercessors, if possible. You'll learn from them and gain confidence. We can learn from every experience, even from prayer times that seem like failures. Our hearts are changed each time we prayerwalk, and, with experience, we learn to sense God's heart more clearly.

Am I Adequate for This Task?

As believers, we often fail to understand the authority that we have in Christ, and because of this we don't exercise our power. We are unsure of ourselves. I know I was. I could identify others who had spiritual authority, but I questioned whether that could be true of me. It helped me to understand some of what the Bible teaches about spiritual authority.[3]

First, all Christians have spiritual authority by virtue of the fact that we have been saved. Our authority flows out of our relationship with Jesus. In Matt. 28:18, Jesus said, "All authority has been given to Me in heaven and on earth." Ephesians 2:6 tells us that "God raised us up with Christ and seated us with Him in the heavenly realms" (NIV). Because we are in Christ, His authority operates in us. We belong to Him, and John 17:18 tells us that just as God sent Jesus, so now Jesus has sent us into the world.

We have the authority to prayerwalk because we are in Christ and He has sent us into the world. As a beginner you can stand on your positional authority while you prayerwalk in public places. For example, if you prayerwalk at a Christian event on public property, you have authority in that place

We have authority to prayerwalk because we are in Christ.

because of your relationship to Christ. That means that your prayers can clear the atmosphere as you pray for the success of the meeting; the enemy has to leave. Positional authority says "My God is bigger than the one you serve."

Second, God graciously bestows an added measure of spiritual authority on some people. You may have noticed, for instance, that some Christians seem particularly gifted to pray about certain things, like healing. God has imparted authority to them. Sometimes, just by being around people who have this imparted authority, we can learn to pray more effectively in their area of giftedness. As you discover areas in which God has given authority, you will become more confident to prayerwalk within your area of giftedness.

Third, we gain spiritual authority by walking in obedience to God. As we grow in obedience, we gain credibility with Him and are given increased spiritual responsibility as a result. This is the authority that Jesus spoke of when He told the story of a servant who was given increasingly greater responsibilities. After the servant proved himself faithful on a small task, his master said, "Well done, good and faithful servant! You have been faithful with a few things; I will put you in charge of many things" (Matt. 25:21 NIV). As we live righteously, we gain increased spiritual authority.

The New Testament emphasizes that personal righteousness is a powerful weapon against evil. For instance, Rom. 12:21 says, "Do not be overcome by evil, but overcome evil with good." That thought is reiterated in 2 Cor. 6:7, where we are to walk "in truthful speech and in the power of God with *weapons* of righteousness in the right hand

and in the left" (NIV, emphasis added). Romans 13:12 expands on this thought: "The night is nearly over, the day is almost here. So let us put aside the deeds of darkness and put on *the armor of light*" (NIV, emphasis added). The Greek word used here for *armor* means *weapon*. Arthur Burk explains, "Light is a weapon that we use against darkness. When you walk into a room, you don't try to strangle darkness. You don't beat it with a club. You don't hang it from a tree with a rope. You bring light in and light overcomes the darkness. . . . Righteousness is an offensive weapon that will bring us spiritual victory."[4]

How does this apply to prayerwalking? First, it means that we must keep ourselves in a close relationship with God. If we're not living in obedience to Christ, our prayerwalking is merely exercise. Obedience enables us to pray effectively.

Second, as we observe the sins and problems in our communities, we remember that those problems are really symptoms of the real problem—unseen demonic powers. Our battle is not against people, but against the demonic forces. But the power of a righteous life puts us in a position to combat the spiritual forces of darkness with light.

So, as a believer, you *do* have the spiritual "credentials" to do this type of ministry. Just be sure that you continue living in obedience to the Lord.

How Will I Know What to Do?

This book will give you the basic resources you need to begin prayerwalking. As you gain experience, God will show you the best prayerwalking strategies for every situation you face.

You'll want to begin by preparing your heart for each prayerwalking experience. Spending time in prayer, self-examination, and Scripture study are simple things you can do to prepare. As you seek God in these ways, the issues that you face and the best prayerwalking response will become clear to you.

One simple strategy for beginning prayerwalking is what I call going in the *opposite spirit*. Here's how it works. Everything has an opposite, and that's true of each virtue and vice as well. For instance, love is the opposite of hatred, self-control is the opposite of self-indulgence, and sharing is the opposite of stealing. A simple way to attack the spiritual issue that underlies a community problem is by prayerwalking in the *opposite* spirit. For example, if you prayerwalk at a public meeting that is likely to be contentious, go in the spirit of peace. When you prayerwalk at a church that has experienced defeat, go in a spirit of joy. Where there is fear, prepare your heart to go in a spirit of faith. You'll see this simple technique applied several times in this book.

As you read the stories that follow, you will notice a specific strategy that was used in each situation. As you gain experience and learn more about prayerwalking, you will gain confidence. Ultimately, however, your strategy will come from God. He will give you direction for each prayerwalk. You'll know what to do.

Are You Ready to Change Your World?

Prayerwalkers are not super-Christians. They're people who believe that God has the power to change their communities, their cities, their nation, and that their prayers can make a difference. There are a lot of things that might discourage you from prayerwalking, but there's one overwhelming reason to do it: God responds to our prayers of faith.

Think of the places that you go each day or each week: a busy street, a bustling office, a sports stadium, a school board meeting, a hospital, a bank, a park, a laundromat. Now imagine those same places transformed by the power of God. Imagine your community, your town, your city, remade by His Spirit.

Can you see it?

Praying on site for your community will increase your awareness of the spiritual need, strengthen your faith in God's power to transform the world, and fill you with hope for people, places, and institutions that now seem beyond hope. Your prayers can make a difference.

Are you ready to change your world?

I will hear what God the Lord will speak,
For He will speak peace. . . .

—Psalm 85:8

CHAPTER ONE

Prayer Letters to the Editor

My First Prayerwalking Assignment

Prayerwalk Challenge

Pray for a local media producer

Prayerwalker Skill

Begin a prayerwalk ministry

While reading the newspaper one morning in 1993, I heard the words, "Prayerwalk the Fort Worth Star-Telegram." The Star-Telegram was the third largest newspaper in Texas and had published a number of articles that seemed antagonistic toward evangelical Christians. The idea of prayerwalking was still quite new to me, and I really didn't know how to go about it. I felt prompted to carry out the task, yet I wondered how to obey. As I asked the Lord what to pray, He began to reveal Scriptures. I compiled them into what became my first prayer focus sheet. Each Scripture seemed like a weapon—a sword.

I had been meeting with six women early each Sunday morning for prayer, Bible study, and accountability. I told them about my project, and they eagerly joined with me. At first, the enemy tried to intimidate us. "What if you get stopped by the police? How will you explain what you are doing on this property?" I could visualize the police ordering us off the property or taking us in for questioning. Of course, the enemy is a liar, and no one would even know, much less care, that we were there.

I felt that our activity needed to be done under the authority of our church, so I asked my pastor, Jim Garlow, who is also my brother, for permission before we began. Though he was doubtful that the editorial policies of the Fort Worth Star-Telegram could be changed, he encouraged us with his blessing. He, too, longed to see a change in the way Christians were portrayed in the newspaper.

Initially, I tried to make the project too big, thinking we needed to drive nearly twenty miles to the newspaper's main office. But the Lord led us to the northeast branch office, which is located in Bedford, near where I lived. We found that the circular, two-story, red brick building was easy to walk around—although I must confess that the first time we went, we were too afraid to get out of the car and brave the cold weather! That first time, we cautiously prayed our Scriptures in the car, wondering what would happen. This was my first prayerwalking experience, and I was a little nervous. We weren't sure just how to go about it, and we certainly didn't want to do anything that would be offensive to others or cause a problem. We prayed for about thirty minutes and then left.

> The first time we went, we were too afraid to get out of the car!

The next week, we went again. We all felt a little more confident this time and agreed to get out of the car and walk. We prayed as we walked around the huge parking lot, which was nearly empty on a Sunday morning. Week by week we felt more freedom to pray the Scriptures aloud and declare truth as God directed. God's compassion for the publisher, editors, and employees of the newspaper began to build in our hearts.

I found that I enjoyed prayerwalking, yet I wondered why God wanted us to pray on site instead of in our homes. He never answered that question, so we simply walked in obedience. Eventually, however, God did answer another question I'd been asking: Why the newspaper? Several years later we learned that, at the time we prayerwalked, that newspaper was considered the most homosexual-friendly newspaper in the nation. We realized, even at the time, that many homosexual people were hired to work at the newspaper, but we only dimly understood the underlying spiritual causes.

Over the weeks that we prayerwalked on that site, my enjoyment of prayerwalking increased. My heart cried out that Isa. 52:7 might be written across the front of the building. In my mind's eye, a large banner was hanging there already (at least in the heavenlies!) proclaiming, "Our God reigns!" After we had prayerwalked there over a six-month period, I sensed that our job was complete and so we stopped going. Within a few weeks, I would see the result of our effort.

The northeast area of Fort Worth was a politically conservative area. Many frustrated people had written letters to the editor of the Star-Telegram, complaining about the flagrantly negative words used to describe Christians, churches, and pro-life activities. Their complaints fell on deaf ears. A few weeks after we concluded our prayerwalks, however, the newspaper's editorial board requested a meeting with Dick Winholt, a respected community leader, to find out why Christians were so angry with them. For three years, God had prompted Pastor Garlow to clip articles from the newspaper and circle the inflammatory words in red. Jim gave his file of clippings to Dick, who used this objective evidence to tactfully explain what needed to be changed.

We were thrilled! God had moved in response to our faithful prayer. He had honored our childlike obedience because *He* wanted to turn the heart of at least one branch of the newspaper.

Shortly after I moved out of the area, one of my prayer partners sent a clipping from the Star-Telegram about a 1996 Promise Keepers event. The article appeared on the front page and included a photo. We rejoiced together that it was an accurate portrayal of the event, without inflammatory quotes from the opposition. Our work had been successful. We obediently prayed, and God answered.

Organizing a Prayerwalk Ministry

Beginning prayerwalkers are often a little bit nervous. Once they begin, however, discomfort usually melts away as they discover the joy of walking and talking with the Lord. If God speaks to you, asking you to pray somewhere on site, don't be afraid to respond. Here are some things you can do to confirm that God is leading you toward a particular assignment and get started in prayerwalking.

Listen for God's Voice

Effective prayerwalking depends on hearing God's voice and responding in obedience. Most people believe God speaks to people today but are not certain how to distinguish His voice. God speaks in our spirit, most commonly by a still, small voice, sometimes described as the sound of a gentle blowing wind (1 Kings 19:12). In Isaiah 30:21, the Lord's voice is described this way:

Your ears shall hear a word behind you, saying,
"This is the way, walk in it,"
Whenever you turn to the right hand
Or whenever you turn to the left.

Jesus said, "My sheep hear My voice, and I know them, and they follow Me" (John 10:27). Barbara Wentroble comments on that verse, "God gives us assurance that we will know the difference between His voice and other voices that may speak to us. '"Yet they will by no means follow a stranger, but will flee from him, for they do not know the voice of strangers'" (John 10:5).[1]

Look for a Specific Assignment

My call to walk the Fort Worth Star-Telegram was a prayer assignment, sometimes called an intercessory call or a burden. One writer describes it this way: "A burden is a deep impression of God's heart and will within our spirit. This burden feels like a weight or a stirring within us that is so strong that we must respond to God so change can come into our lives or environment. This is how intercession begins."[2]

When you receive an assignment, respond in obedience and trust your inner prompting as you pray. God will use those promptings to reveal the areas that need prayer and strategies for overcoming the enemy. Cindy Jacobs explains that when the Lord is speaking to us, "an answer from within our hearts will cry, 'Yes, that is God speaking to me.' We will *resonate* with the Word. This is what I mean by a witness in your spirit"[3]

Confirm God's Leading by His Written Word

Ask God for confirmation of what you believe you have heard. The Bible is our only completely reliable standard. God does not contradict His written Word when He speaks to us. That means we must study the Word to know both its teachings and the character of God revealed in the Word. Is what you hear contrary to His nature? Does it sound like something God would say? If necessary, study the issue carefully using a concordance or other Bible reference tool.

Use common sense. The Bible doesn't address everything we find in our modern society so don't worry if you don't find a verse about computers or cars in the Bible. It is also a good idea to confirm your own

> With practice you will learn to distinguish God's voice from that of others.

study by checking your findings with mature prayer partners. Describe what you think God has said and allow them to prayerfully respond, either with confirmation that it sounds right or that there is a caution in their spirit. Mature believers can keep us grounded in the Word by helping us to confirm what we've heard. With practice you will learn to distinguish God's voice from that of others, yourself or even the enemy. Do not hesitate to confirm and reconfirm a message that you believe is from God.

Having said that, be careful about whom you ask for confirmation and evaluate their responses as well. God does say things that are contrary to our natural, human way of thinking. Be careful not to limit God (John 4:23–24). Guard against a religious mind-set that assumes that God's actions should always make sense (1 Cor. 1:18–25). On some rare occasions, we can be confident that we have heard God's voice, even if nobody else agrees. Like John the Baptist, sometimes we walk alone in what we know. Yet we do so humbly, after checking as thoroughly as we can.

Connect with a Leader

It is advantageous for a church to have a designated prayerwalk leader who can oversee or organize prayerwalks as an ongoing ministry. Permission should be obtained from appropriate church leaders before undertaking prayerwalking. One of the keys to an effective prayerwalk ministry is ongoing communication. Coordinate your efforts with church leaders. They'll let you know what the needs of the church are and help you decide when prayerwalking might be God's strategy.

Be sure to share appropriate information regarding prayerwalks with your pastor. Also, connect with prayer leaders and intercessors from other congregations to gain a greater understanding of what God is doing in your area.

Determine the Membership of the Team

Next, determine whom to involve in your prayerwalk. You might go alone, but I usually like to invite others who are also interested in prayer. A good way to invite someone to prayerwalk is to ask, "Is this something God wants you to do?"

For those who are interested, consider offering some training before setting out. You will want to be sure that everyone understands the purpose of the prayerwalk, what you will do, and what things to avoid. This training might include conducting a prayerwalk at your church. Churches are great places to learn because they are familiar territories and do not involve travel.

Prepare the Team for the Prayerwalk

Before you begin your prayerwalk, pray for protection and guidance. Give those who join you for the walk brief instructions on where you are going and what the focus of your prayer will be. Provide maps or any other information that they'll need to move about the area. You might distribute a prayer focus sheet (like the one at the end of this chapter) that will assist team members in praying and may trigger their own spontaneous prayers. Be natural, and keep your eyes open as you pray.

One prayerwalker recalled his first prayerwalk this way: "It requires simple faith to step out of my security zone and into the world. Have a simple belief that God is with you and that He will use you. Ask God, 'Show me what You want me to do for them, in Your name.' I walked with a song of praise in my heart not knowing exactly what to do but trusting, through obedience, that an opportunity would come."

Record Your Results

Take note of what happened on your prayerwalk and what happens after. Watch for evidence of God's work, and record those results, but don't exaggerate. We want to be credible in what we claim. When we prayerwalk in the world, God peels off our own layers of deception. We pray for His truth to be established, and that begins with us.

After you've prayerwalked, keep your eye on the news to watch for results. If your city has experienced an increase in the murder rate and you prayerwalk in the opposite spirit, praying life-giving Scriptures over the community, recheck the crime statistics some months after the prayerwalk. Monitor the spiritual climate of an area. Talk to city leaders. Watch for the atmosphere to change in that location. It is a great encouragement to see God's answers to our prayers.

When we act on the prayer assignments that God has confirmed in our spirit, we pray with great authority. Amazing things can happen as a result. Psalm 29 declares that the voice of the Lord shakes, breaks, and births. That can also happen from the power of His voice spoken through us. My husband, Keat, reflected on that sound in a poem. Listen for His voice.

His Voice

Thoughts from Psalm 29
Do you hear it?
Quiet, listen now;
Just above the sound of
Breaking waves
And running tide...
His Voice?

Do you hear it?
In the thunder
Powerful, full of majesty
Breaking cedars
Dividing flames of fire. . .
His Voice?

Do you hear it?
Shaking the wilderness

The wilderness of Kadesh
Causing the deer to give birth
Stripping the forest bare
While people in the temple shout "Glory"?

From His throne room
Where He sits forever
Giving strength to His people
Blessing His people with peace
He whispers, "Listen" . . .
Hear the Voice of I AM!

—Keat Wade

PRAYER ACTION LIST
How to Organize a Prayerwalk

❑ Listen for the voice of God, directing you to pray for a certain location.

❑ Confirm that leading through the Word and from the affirmation of mature believers.

❑ Obtain permission for your prayerwalk from a spiritual authority such as your pastor if you represent a church or other organization.

❑ Gather people who have some interest in learning about prayerwalking.

❑ Train and equip them using resources such as this book.

❑ Stay connected with your leaders and your team. Communicate frequently.

❑ Practice prayerwalking at your church.

❑ Gather the team for prayer and instructions before setting out.

❑ Debrief after each prayerwalk, asking, "What did God say?"

❑ Share information with appropriate leaders such as pastor, prayer leaders, or other spiritual leaders in your city.

❑ Watch for news reports or other evidence that confirm the results of your prayerwalk and report them accurately.

PRAYER FOCUS
First Prayerwalk

Before You Start

Joshua 1:3: "Every place the sole of your foot will tread upon I have given you."

We take authority in Jesus name because You have said every place the sole of our foot treads You will give to us.

Psalm 24:4: "He who has clean hands and a pure heart, Who has not lifted up his soul to an idol, Nor sworn deceitfully."

We ask for clean hands and a clean heart.

Ephesians 5:26: ". . . sanctify and cleanse her with the washing of water by the word."

Father, we ask You to cleanse us with the washing of water by the Word. Help us to speak the Word over our territory.

During the Prayerwalk

Psalm 119:45: "And I will walk in liberty, For I seek Your precepts."

Father, because we have asked for clean hearts, we come with earned authority. As we walk about, cause us to be free to see [the city] as You see it. Show us the path You want us to take.

Acts 26:18: ". . . open their eyes, in order to turn them from darkness to light, and from the power of Satan to God, that they may receive forgiveness of sins and an inheritance among those who are sanctified by faith in Me."

We pray eyes will be open. We pray that people will turn from darkness.

1 Peter 2:9: "But you are a chosen generation, a royal priesthood, a holy nation, His own special people, that you may proclaim the praises of Him who called you out of darkness into His marvelous light."

Lord, we ask You to call our neighbors into the light.

The people who know their God will
display strength and take action.
                    —Daniel 11:32

CHAPTER TWO

The Day God
Fixed the
Media Truck

A Solo Prayerwalk

Prayerwalk Challenge

Pray for a protest rally

Prayerwalker Skill

Discern God's leading

I heard on the radio that a rally would be held the next day at the War Memorial, near the San Diego Zoo. Protestors had planned to condemn the possible impeachment of President Bill Clinton and the impeachment proceedings that were then taking place in the U. S. House of Representatives. People favoring impeachment were also mobilizing to make a strong showing at the same rally. The situation had the potential to become an ugly confrontation, and national media planned to cover the rally if it proved to be newsworthy.

I value the right to peacefully assemble, a precious freedom for

Americans, yet I sensed trouble. I was concerned that this particular rally would contribute further to unrighteousness in our city. I quickly asked God whom I should invite to prayerwalk and heard, "No one; there isn't time. Go alone."

Later that day I found the War Memorial, a tired, drab-looking building dedicated to all war veterans. I parked my car at random, not realizing that it would later prove to be a strategic location.

I felt God's presence and heard, "Here."

Scanning the area, I asked God where to walk and pray. I didn't sense a clear direction, so I started by walking down a hallway, praying for truth and righteousness to be established (Ps. 85:10–13). I looked into several meeting rooms and anointed the front doors with oil. Puzzled that I could not sense a definite leading from God, I exited through the side door and then prayerwalked my way around the building.

As I approached the front patio area, I felt God's presence and heard, "Here." At that point, I felt led to shift from intercession to worship. I took my seat on a bench near a flagpole, with a beautiful view of the distant mountains. I worshiped for twenty minutes until I felt a release in my spirit. Thinking that my task was finished, I returned to my car.

That's when I discovered that my keys were locked inside the car! Knowing it would be dark within the hour, I hurried back to the Memorial to find a telephone. I found someone working in an office and asked for a phone book so I could locate a locksmith. The first name I saw was A Anointed Locksmith. "That's the one," I thought and dialed the number. The locksmith said he would be there in forty-five minutes.

I waited by my car, asking God why I was standing there in an all-but-empty parking lot. Just then, a van topped with a satellite dish lumbered in and parked between my car and the Memorial. Two men got out of the truck. I noticed that it was from the NBC television station in Burbank, a suburb of Los Angeles. They had driven more than two hours from Burbank to cover the rally!

"Oops, this is going to be a big event," I thought.

As the men walked away from the truck, I was left standing just a few yards from the equipment that could relay news from our city all over the world. The opportunity was too good to pass up. As the men walked toward the building, I slipped across the parking lot, anointing oil in hand. I anointed the front, middle, and rear of the truck, declaring, "Only good news will be published from this truck," based on Isa. 52:7.

A moment later, I returned to my car. The men were looking over the patio area where I had just worshiped, discussing camera angles for tomorrow. I smiled with satisfaction, realizing that God had led me to exactly the right place.

Just after the men returned to their truck and drove away, the "anointed locksmith" arrived with a big fish sign on his truck. When he asked what I was doing there, I explained that I had been praying over the area where a rally was going to be held the next day—praying peace, truth, and righteousness for our city (Ps. 122:7; Ps. 51:6). After he unlocked my car door, we continued talking about the things of God. The occasion became an opportunity to unite in prayer as this African-American gentleman stood with me in agreement for righteousness to prevail on that spot.

At noon the next day, I happened to watch the news. The news-caster appeared flustered. "We are having trouble with our satellite feed from the protest rally," she said. "We will have a report in a few minutes." I watched the scrambled television picture in stunned amazement. The protest was to have been the lead story.

Ten minutes later, the satellite feed was restored and the field cor-respondent gave her report against a backdrop of mass confusion. We couldn't see or hear any of the speakers, but the reporter described the scene. The rally organizers had not anticipated the number of counter demonstrators that had mobilized in support of impeachment proceed-ings. The two groups screamed defiantly at each other, but their angry words were not broadcast to the world.

Later that day, the national news programs barely mentioned the San Diego rally, and the ineffective protest did not spark further national demonstrations. The enemy had a lot up his sleeve, but this was one scrimmage he lost.

Developing Discernment

Discernment is insight. To have discernment is to have keen perception, good judgment, or to distinguish the truth. We often use the word *sense* when speaking of spiritual discernment. To sense is to have an impression or to be aware of something. Carefully evaluating the things that we sense often enables us to see what is "wrong with this picture," to see the situation as God sees it. That's discernment.

It's important to develop discernment because its opposite is deception. When we lack discernment, we lose effectiveness as prayerwalkers. Author Cindy Tosto explains, "there are two goals when prayerwalking: (1) to pray blessings upon the land and people who surround you; and (2) to discern and remove the enemy and his influence. . . . As you praise the Lord and pray blessings for others, the Light of Jesus shines where you are. Wherever there is light, the darkness cannot remain."[1]

The Bible itself admonishes us to recognize God's wisdom and truth. The Bible speaks of Christians as those "who have trained themselves to recognize the difference between right and wrong and then do what is right" (Heb. 5:14 NLT). Another translation makes the point even more clearly, referring to believers as "those whose senses and mental faculties are trained by practice to discriminate and distinguish between what is morally good and noble and what is evil and contrary either to divine or human law" (Heb 5:14 AMP). Proverbs 15:21 advises, "Folly is joy to him who is destitute of discernment, but a man of understanding walks uprightly." The Amplified Bible adds "making straight his course." And David reminds us, "Behold, You desire truth in the inward parts [of me], And in the hidden part You will make me to know wisdom" (Ps. 51:6).

> The body of Christ desperately needs greater discernment in these days.

I believe that the body of Christ desperately needs greater discernment in these days. The church cannot expect the government, military, or police to protect us totally. We need to be "as shrewd as snakes and as innocent as doves" (Matt. 10:16 NIV). Often, desperation is what drives us to discernment. I carry a great burden for the Church because I see how much it has suffered. I believe our lives depend on being discerning. Here are some practical ways that you can develop or increase your discernment, a valuable skill for prayerwalking.

Apply the Word

When you need wisdom in any situation, look first to God's written Word. Some situations are very easy to assess because they can be measured against our standard for discernment, the Word of God. Scripture is the plumbline for determining the rightness of anything. Any act or practice that violates the counsel of the Word must be rejected. You need look no further.

Ask God

It may sound obvious, but it is an often-overlooked principle: God gives discernment to those who ask for it. When you prayerwalk, pray for guidance about where to go and how to approach the situation. As James reminds us, "If any of you lacks wisdom, he should ask God, who gives generously to all without finding fault, and it will be given to him" (James 1:5 NIV).

Observe Mature Christians

Look around for people who have an obvious gift of discernment. I like to be around them to listen to what they share and to spend time praying with them. When a mature believer states some spiritual truth, I frequently ask, "How do you know that?" They have been very honest with me. Learning about their impressions helps me with mine.

Keep Your Heart Clear

Discernment comes from having a close connection with God, and that depends upon having a pure heart. We need to maintain clean hearts if we are to be people of discernment.[2] Daily life seems to bring a lot of corrosion, so it's essential that we clear our hearts before prayerwalking. To do that, ask God to remind you of anything that displeases Him so you can repent of it. And remember, when you ask God to convict your heart, He will! The experience can be humbling, but it is always rewarding.

God may reveal some great fault to you, or He may go straight for the little things that are so easy for us to ignore—selfish attitudes, little bits of dishonesty, unkind words or thoughts. My husband and I make it a habit to search our hearts in a spirit of repentance while on the way to a prayerwalk or as soon as we arrive. When in a group, we do this silently. I'm often amazed at the things God brings to my mind. Usually it's something that I'd considered insignificant and forgotten.

As soon as He pulls it up on my heart's screen, I say, "Forgive me Lord. I am sorry. I receive the cleansing of Your blood." Our heart's cry should be the same as David's: "Create in me a clean heart" (Ps. 51:10). Purity of heart is essential for effective intercession.

> Who may stand in His holy place? He who has clean hands and a pure heart, Who has not lifted up his soul to an idol, Nor sworn deceitfully. He shall receive blessing from the LORD, And righteousness from the God of his salvation. This is . . . the generation of those who seek Him, Who seek Your face. (Ps. 24:3b–6)

Clean hands represent right actions. A pure heart indicates pure motives. I like to think of the heart as a satellite dish that needs to be pointed toward the satellite in outer space in order to receive a signal. In the same way, our hearts need to be pointed toward God and open to Him if we are to receive discernment. To develop discernment, we need to have our hearts aimed with pinpoint accuracy in the right direction.

Repentance is what keeps our hearts aligned with God. It brings increased perception and discernment. As fallible human beings, we have the need to repent often. Keeping our hearts right with God gives us power against the enemy. You've heard of frequent flyer miles? I call this frequent repenter miles!

Applying Discernment

Gaining discernment is important, but discernment must also be applied. Knowing the truth is not enough; we must act upon it. Let's review the story of the media truck to see how to apply discernment. Here are ways in which discernment applies to prayerwalking.

Sense Why to Pray

When I heard the report of the protest rally on the radio, I sensed that the situation needed prayer. I asked God for increased discernment and questioned Him, "What do you want me to understand or discern?" Often, I am not sure why a situation needs prayer. In this case, there was a national political conflict. Yet I sensed something deeper. Later, I was to learn of a national scheme to use our area as a springboard to promote the homosexual agenda. The goal was something bigger than supporting an embattled president. This was a strategic battle with consequences that would have affected the whole nation.

I am usually reluctant to move forward in prayer for things that are beyond my human knowledge until I gain some understanding. However, I walk in obedience and step out in faith, knowing that His instruction will come. It takes faith to step forward with only a word or phrase. I often hear God say only, "This is important. Pray." My response is always, "Pray what?" Often, I get no further instruction. In those cases, I rely on these general guidelines, which are always on target:

- Ask God for increased discernment.
- If the subject of prayer is a person, pray for protection and exposure of the enemy's schemes.
- If it is a situation, pray for truth, righteousness, and justice.

Sense When to Pray

When the protest rally was announced, I sensed that I was to pray that day. At public events, it is usually best to pray before security is in place or the area is cordoned off. I often visit the site of such events one to three days before the event begins. That way, I have greater freedom to move around. Also, there are fewer distractions. When I pray before an event, I can be relaxed and not have to worry about the commotion around me. Later I can attend the event to witness it, not to prayerwalk.

When I am led to prayerwalk, I try to get a sense of how long I am to pray. I pray until I feel a release in my spirit. That usually comes as a sudden inclination to celebrate, and sometimes I get the thought to go get a bite to eat.

Sense Where to Pray

When possible, I do visual research on site in preparation for a prayerwalk. I read the signs, plaques, cornerstones, and overhead symbols. I find out what the building is dedicated to and why. If it is dedicated to a righteous purpose, I pray what is righteous into being. If it's dedicated to a wicked purpose, I pray for redemption. That usually involves praying in the opposite spirit, such as praying in the spirit of humility versus the spirit of pride, purity in place of pornography, or sacrificial sharing instead of greed.

At the War Memorial, I went inside and then circled the building before I sensed that I was to linger in the front patio. I hadn't noticed that patio area before. Don't ignore small nudgings of the Spirit.

Sense What to Pray

While I explored the War Memorial building, I was praying for truth, righteousness, justice, and peace to be established. I continued in this vein while circling the building. When I arrived at the patio, I asked God what to pray and heard, "Worship." My sense of God's presence was strong. I felt strengthened from being in His presence.

I'm reminded of Ps. 23:5. "Thou preparest a table for me in the presence of mine enemies. . ." (KJV). When I think of that verse, I picture sitting at a banquet table with wonderful, relaxed fellowship. Yes, in front of the enemy. And, yes, God does turn adversity into an adventure!

Sense Who Should Pray

When forming a prayerwalk team, act upon your discernment and allow for trial and error. God always knows how many He needs. More than one person might have drawn attention when I walked around the media truck. Sometimes one or two people have more freedom to move around than a large group would. God frequently uses small numbers—three to six.

I am always amazed at the power of one. Sometimes I ask God, "If You, God, only need one, why do You need anybody at all? Is this really necessary?" The answer is that God needs us to pray because He has sovereignly chosen this method to accomplish His will. He doesn't have to explain why. Just walk in obedience, and pray when He asks you to pray.

Watch for clues that will confirm the results of your discernment and your prayerwalking. God wants to encourage you, so you will often see results. Whenever I do, I am strengthened with renewed hope. I have prayed the Word, which is food for my soul. I have learned what is on God's heart, so I have had intimacy with Him. I have new information because of my research, so my mind is enlarged. I meet new friends, sometimes anointed ones, so my relationships are broadened.

What an adventure!

PRAYER ACTION LIST
How to Develop Discernment

❑ Apply God's Word to the situation that you face and the discernment that you sense.

❑ Ask God for increased discernment.

❑ Identify those who have discernment, listen to their words, and ask, "How do you know that?"

❑ Maintain close fellowship with God by repenting frequently.

❑ Allow for trial and error, but don't hesitate to act upon your discernment.

❑ When you prayerwalk, try to sense why, when, where, what, and with whom to pray.

❑ Watch for clues that will confirm what you have discerned.

PRAYER FOCUS
Truth and Discernment

Psalm 51:6: "Behold, You desire truth in the inward parts, And in the hidden part You will make me to know wisdom."

Father, we ask for increased wisdom and a desire for truth.

Proverbs 15:21: "Folly is joy to him who is destitute of discernment, But a man of understanding walks uprightly."

We repent of those occasions when we have entertained deception. We pray for increased discernment and the understanding to walk uprightly.

Psalm 85:10–13: "Mercy and truth have met together; Righteousness and peace have kissed. Truth shall spring out of the earth, And righteousness shall look down from heaven. Yes, the Lord will give what is good; And our land will yield its increase. Righteousness will go before Him, And shall make His footsteps our pathway."

Father, we ask You to establish greater truth and righteousness in (name a person, place, or situation).

John 17:17: "Sanctify them by Your truth. Your word is truth."

Father, sanctify us by Your truth as we pray Your word.

Hebrews 5:14 (NIV): "But solid food is for the mature, who by constant use have trained themselves to distinguish good from evil."

Cause us to discern good from evil.

So I will strengthen them in the Lord . . .
they shall walk up and down in His name.
—Zechariah 10:12

CHAPTER THREE

Lemon Grove 91945

Prayerwalking an Entire Community

Prayerwalk Challenge

Prayerwalk an entire community

Prayerwalker Skill

Pray the Word

The first zip code in the San Diego area to be completely prayerwalked was 91945. That zip code represents the three-square-mile city of Lemon Grove, California, population 24,700. It is located twenty minutes east of San Diego.

I had been teaching prayerwalk classes as part of the prayer ministry of our church, Skyline Wesleyan, then located in Lemon Grove. Our normal pattern was to have twenty minutes of training and then to travel somewhere to prayerwalk in a particular location. Before starting out, we would pray, repenting of our sins so we would have clean hands and a pure heart. We also prayed to put on the armor of God (Eph. 6:10–18). Finally, we prayed for God's orders for that particular walk.

We started in the place where we had spiritual authority—our church. We prayerwalked our church property praying Psalm 91, declaring God's protection over the property and our congregation. From there we fanned out across Lemon Grove, concentrating on one section of the city at a time.

> By September 1997, we had covered the entire city with prayer.

After several training exercises around our church property, we decided to venture to the Lemon Grove city hall, which also included a regional county sheriff's office, the city's protective agency. This time, we felt that God was directing the ladies to pray together and the men to pray together. The groups walked in opposite directions, circling the building several times. We prayed to be hidden so that we could carry out our prayerwalk without being disturbed. A young sheriff's officer looked out the window once but didn't seem to notice anything unusual about ten people walking in an empty parking lot at 8:00 P.M.

Locating the right map to use for prayerwalking is sometimes a challenge. One of our members obtained a city map from the fire department so we could mark each street in red after it had been prayerwalked. The map hung on the wall in a room used by intercessors, pastors, and church board members. The city slowly turned red as we completed our mission. It was interesting that the map also showed the location of all fire hydrants in the city. Maybe that was a sign of things to come—except that we wanted God to start fires of revival, not put them out!

We prayerwalked in the city one Saturday morning each month for about three hours. By September 1997, we had prayerwalked for about six months and had covered the entire city with prayer. We completed this assignment using no more than ten or twelve prayerwalkers at a time, praying in assigned areas in teams of two or three. We enjoyed our time with the Lord so much that we hated to see this assignment end. We sensed His Presence faithfully with us throughout the city.

On each prayerwalk we prayed the Word using Steve Hawthorn's booklet, *Prompts for Prayerwalkers—Seven Ways to Pray from God's Word for Your World*. It's a small booklet, easy to read while walking. It includes a Scripture followed by a written prayer that acts as a prompt for praying and walking. It was easy to pray for several hours this way, with eyes wide open looking around as we walked.

We also prayed *search and rescue* prayers. We asked God to show us who He was pursuing and to sweep away the clutter in order to find those who are lost (Luke 15:4, 8, 24). One day we saw six different people sweeping; we understood that as a prophetic sign of God sweeping the city with His Word.

Next, we prayed *send Your Word* prayers, asking for His Word to go forth and to "speak . . . with great boldness" (Act 4:29 NIV). A prayerwalker named Lisa took this to heart and boldly walked up to a house where it was obvious that people were at home. She asked the young woman who answered the door, Catalina, if she had any prayer requests. Lisa's prayer moved Catalina deeply and demonstrated God's love for her. It also provided a stunning encouragement to Catalina's aunt, who had just returned from an all-night prayer meeting where she had prayed for Catalina's salvation.

The last area of the city that we prayerwalked contained an adult nightclub that featured nude dancers. Not so coincidentally, the agenda of the men's ministry that Saturday addressed the issue of pornography. Simultaneously, God was cleaning up hearts in the church as well as the city.

Weeks before we went, I encouraged the team to worship (the highest form of spiritual warfare) any time we drove past the adult video store and the adult nightclub during the week. I told them the story of Mrs. Johnson, an elderly, wheelchair-bound lady who, along with another woman, had led several prayerwalks in front of both businesses five years earlier. They were so successful that a judge shut down the video store for a few days; then the matter was supposed to go to court. The community hoped that the store would be shut down permanently. Further encouragement came when the adult club was closed after a fire

> **We asked God to sweep away the clutter in order to find those who are lost.**

in 1992. Then Mrs. Johnson died, and the other prayer leader moved out of the area. That brought us to the present, 1997.

Community people had been naïve about the process of change and underestimated the tenacious hold of the pornographic industry on the city. The nightclub had recently reopened and both businesses were again thriving. I wanted our team members to know the history of these places as they prayed. We were continuing Mrs. Johnson's walk and adding to the prayers of others who were concerned about those businesses. The work was not finished.

> This story is not finished.
> We continue to pray for that area of the city.

I also mentioned that it would be nice if we had some connection inside the bar, a way to monitor the spiritual progress as we prayed and perhaps build a connection with the dancing girls. I noticed a stricken look on the face of one of our prayerwalkers. During the summer a woman named Dawn had joined us for several walks. I knew that she had been burdened for her wayward daughter. Later, she told me that she would not accompany us on our final walk. I asked, "Is that where your daughter works?"

"Yes," she said. "It would be too hard on me, but I am fully supportive of the walk. I also want to be affirming of Louisa." She was concerned Louisa might become estranged from her if she saw her walking outside. I supported her decision and valued the opportunity to open a spiritual lifeline with her daughter. How profound and sad that we already had a connection to that vile business from within our own church. We went on our Saturday walk praying both for the community as a whole and for a particular young woman named Louisa.

We were delighted when Louisa accepted Christ in August of that year. Our prayers had been answered! Soon after, Louisa witnessed the baptism of her brother at our church, and Pastor Jim Garlow saw her raise her hand to receive healing from drug addiction. In December she went into treatment and spent Christmas clean, joyful, and talking about the Lord.

But the story did not turn out as we'd expected. Louisa checked out of the facility after twenty-six days of a twenty-eight-day Christian treatment program. Again her mother called intercessors to pray. The next day

Louisa died of an overdose of heroin after a yearlong battle with that drug. Her death hit us hard. This was one intercessory battle we lost.

The funeral was held at our church, and Dawn graciously invited Louisa's friends from the nightclub to attend. Before the funeral began, we prayerwalked the sanctuary, praying for the salvation of those attending. Pastor Garlow powerfully presented the gospel to the several hundred people in attendance, among them the managers, employees, and dancers at the nightclub. We had begun our prayerwalk hoping to see the adult nightclub closed. We never expected that the nightclub would come to our church!

This story is not finished. We continue to pray for that area of the city. We don't want the businesses to move but to be closed by prayer and by the salvation of the owners and patrons. During and following the city prayerwalk we gathered data on the city. Before our walk, in 1996 and 1997, the newspaper reported six drive-by shootings. After we prayerwalked there was nothing at all printed about such incidents in Lemon Grove. Drive-by shootings have been replaced by drive-by prayers as we continue to intercede for our community.

At the city prayer breakfast, we were able to tell Mayor Mary Sessoms that on the next day, we would complete our prayerwalk of the entire city. The mayor expressed delight and gratitude for our intercession. When we completed our final walk, the Word had been prayed on every street of our city.

Learning to Pray the Word

The purpose of prayer is not to convince God what to do or tell Him something He doesn't know. Prayer is more like a two-way conversation between friends. As we come to understand God's heart and study His Word, He reveals to us His plans for people and regions. Though God is sovereign, He has chosen "to work on the earth with and through us, not independently of us. He honors this decision in every way."[1] When we pray Scripture back to God, we honor Him by aligning ourselves with His plans. Here's how to pray the Word, using Scripture as you prayerwalk.

Pray the Word over Yourself in Preparation

We prepare for praying the Word by praying Scripture over ourselves to purify our hands and hearts. Using the Scripture in this way is like taking a cleansing shower. I like to pray that "He might sanctify and cleanse her [the Church—you and me] with the washing of water by the word" (Eph. 5:26). I personalize that verse by praying, "Sanctify and cleanse *me* by the washing of water by the Word." When we first pray the Word over ourselves, we then prayerwalk with earned authority to pray over our church or city. As the church is cleansed, more and more people will be set free. Psalm 119:45 (NIV) says, "I will walk about in freedom for I have sought out your precepts."

Pray that, as a prayerwalker, the very Scriptures you pray over others will wash you clean. This is one dramatic way in which the enemy is defeated. When problems arise within our children or families, cities, regions, or nation, we pray the Father's heart by praying His own Scripture back to Him. We are cleansed in the process so the crud of the world and lies of the enemy are exposed, even to ourselves, and removed. This preparation brings increased discernment so that we can pray more on target.

Select Scripture to Use on Your Prayerwalk

For our group, it was awkward at first to use Scripture in prayer. Having a prayer guide helped us become more comfortable, and we soon found that saying the Scripture out loud helped also. As we got used to our own voices, it brought a powerful release to our faith. Speaking Scripture is wonderful.

We began with the prayer that Jesus taught us to pray, the Lord's Prayer. At first it was awkward to pray the Lord's Prayer in that way, but it began to flow as we felt His Presence join us. We not only prayed for our neighbors but also included ourselves by praying for repentance and purity. I felt that this pleased God. We prayed:

- *Our Father in heaven . . .* "We come near You in heaven by the way made by Jesus. We come near our neighbors on earth that a way would be opened for You in their lives as well as ours."

- *Hallowed be Your name . . .* "You are so worthy of praise for what You are already doing in their lives. Here is our request: Reveal who You are by name."

It often took at least twenty minutes just to get through the Lord's Prayer. Never had we experienced this familiar Scripture in this way. The Word came alive.

It took a while to learn how to pray using the Beatitudes. It's not easy to pray blessings because we're so used to praying requests. Yet we stayed focused and asked God to show us how to bless as well as bring petitions. Steve Hawthorne says that when we pray a blessing, "faith speaks words which match God's own desire for the destiny of particular people."[2]

You may wonder what Scripture to use for the focus of your prayers. That depends on your answer to this question: What do you want the prayer to address for the sake of God's kingdom? Many Psalms are prayers already, so it is easy to put them in your own words. They include songs of praise, confession, and lament. The book of Isaiah is another good place to start. Pick a few Scriptures that are meaningful to you and try saying them as prayers. You will begin to settle on some that are more comfortable for you. Print up a sheet of three to five Scriptures and underline words or phrases that you want to catch your eye as you are walking. Take it with you and use it like a cue sheet to prompt your prayers.

Notice and Record the Scriptures God Emphasizes

Our group noticed that God sometimes placed special emphasis on certain Scriptures. They became His Word for that day. Sometimes He applied the same Scripture different ways depending on the circumstances. When we prayed the Scriptures that the Holy Spirit had emphasized for a given situation, our prayer was more effective. We would meditate on a phrase or word until we felt a release. If you ask Him, the Holy Spirit will arm you with exactly the right sword to swing.

On one prayerwalk God revealed to me that "Blessed are those who mourn, for they shall be comforted" (Matt 5:4) was to be prayed for men or woman with anger problems involved in domestic violence. We had walked by houses where we sensed there was chaos and perhaps violence, and I never felt satisfied with what we prayed. Yet He revealed to me that they were mourning their many losses, isolation, and feelings of powerlessness. We blessed them, saying, "Upon them we speak peace upon anger, solace upon anguish, and Father God's own Presence unlocking prisons of loneliness." There is nothing like having a Bible study in the middle of the street!

Make a record of these verses to remember them. Don't forget to date your entries. This will be invaluable later when you review the events in your community that were affected by your prayers. Your entries become part of God's spiritual calendar for your church or city.

Provide opportunities to evaluate by asking the team, "What did you learn?" I usually ask teams to report back for a short briefing after prayerwalks. This provides an opportunity to record the Scriptures used and any impressions that were made. Sometimes team members turn in a brief written report. I repeatedly ask them, "What did God *say?*" to reinforce the necessity of listening to God with the expectation that He does have something to say directly to us.

Praying the Word helps us to be more effective in our praying and to persevere. We learn to focus on the big picture—the need for purity in the Body of Christ and the need for greater unity in order to affect an entire region.

PRAYER ACTION LIST
How to Pray the Word

❑ Determine the prayer focus. Answer the question "What do we want the prayer to address for Kingdom purposes?"

❑ Look for Scriptures that express the focus in God's words.

❑ Print out an easy-to-read prayer focus sheet in outline form and underline important words and phrases.

❑ Pray Scripture over yourself before setting out. Pray for purity, unity, protection, and guidance.

❑ Pray with your eyes open and keep prayers in a normal tone without drawing attention to yourself.

❑ Use the prayer focus sheet and be sensitive to the Holy Spirit's promptings, which might trigger other prayers.

❑ Evaluate the prayerwalk by asking one another "What did you learn?" and "What did God say?"

❑ Record your experience and any observed results.

PRAYER FOCUS
Praying the Word

For Seeking God's Heart

Proverbs 19:20: "Listen to counsel and receive instruction, That you may be wise. . . ."

We declare our need for Your perspective and words in order to establish Your purpose.

Psalm 119:130 (AMP): "The entrance and unfolding of Your words give light; their unfolding gives understanding (discernment and comprehension) to the simple."

Unfold Your words to us that we may have light, understanding, and discernment.

For Thanking the Holy Spirit

Hebrews 4:12 (NASB): "For the word of God is living and active and sharper than any two-edged sword, and piercing as far as the division of soul and spirit, of both joints and marrow, and able to judge the thoughts and intentions of the heart."

We thank you, Holy Spirit, for making the Word of God our weapon.

Jeremiah 23:28–29: "He who has My word, let him speak My word faithfully. . . . Is not My word like a fire?" says the Lord, "And like a hammer that breaks the rock in pieces?"

Thank You, that Your word in my mouth is like a fire and a hammer.

For Praising God

Jeremiah 1:12 (NASB); Then the Lord said to me, ". . . I am watching over My word to perform it."

We praise You, God, that You are watching over Your Word.

Isaiah 55:11 (NASB): "So will My word be which goes forth from My mouth; It shall not return to Me empty, Without accomplishing what I desire, And without succeeding in the matter for which I sent it."

We praise You that Your words accomplish and succeed in the desires of Your heart.

John 15:7: "If you abide in Me, and My words abide in You, you will ask what you desire, and it shall be done for you."

We declare that we abide in You and Your words abide in us, therefore, when we pray according to Your Word, it will be done.

For Raising up the Shield of Faith

Romans 10:17: "So then faith comes by hearing, and hearing by the word of God."

As I hear Your word prayed, my faith rises.

Ephesians 6:16: (NASB): ". . . taking up the shield of faith with which you will be able to extinguish all the flaming arrows of the evil one."

I thank You that faith is a shield to me, extinguishing all the flaming arrows of the enemy.

How beautiful . . . are the feet of him . . .
who publishes peace. . . .
　　　　　　　—Isaiah 52:7 (AMP)

CHAPTER FOUR

Hidden in Plain View

Prayerwalking the Republican Convention

Prayerwalk Challenge

Pray for a political convention

Prayerwalker Skill

Find prayer assignments in the newspaper

Shortly after moving from Dallas to San Diego in January of 1996, I learned that my new hometown would host the Republican National Convention that summer. I'd never attended a national convention but avidly watched both the Republican and Democratic conventions every four years. I like to study history, and I see politics as history in the making. To attend either convention would have been a thrill.

When I heard the news, I felt prompted to prayerwalk in preparation for the convention. To prayerwalk the beautiful San

Diego Convention Center, overlooking a gorgeous harbor, seemed like one divine assignment!

Since I was new in the area and hadn't met many local intercessors yet, I invited a group of willing "pray-ers" to participate in several prayerwalks. We explored the building, praying for truth and righteousness to be established (Ps. 85:10–13). We rode the escalators and visited the convention floor during the construction of the speaker's platform. Every square inch of the convention center was carefully prepared to accommodate the anticipated throngs of delegates, guests, and television broadcasters.

> With San Diego spread before us, we prayed boldly for the peace of the city.

Protesters were mobilizing too. The police department had determined that protests could be staged in a parking lot beside the Convention Center. We prayed over this lot several times, declaring confusion upon the enemy (Ps. 35:26). While we valued the right of all people to express their views, we were hopeful that the protests would not become divisive or even violent. The police prepared well for the situation and did an excellent job. Few protesters assembled, and those that came drew little attention to themselves.

Every day I carefully read the newspaper to find evidence of emerging plans and asked God to show me what needed prayer. When I read that ten thousand media people would attend the convention, I was struck by the great opportunity we had to pray for the national and international media. Our group circled in prayer around the area where the media vans would be located. Most of the media representatives would be lodged at the Marriott Hotel, next door to the Convention Center. I wept my way through the towers of the hotel as God poured what was on His heart into mine. My heart was broken as He revealed their loneliness and isolation. Our last major prayerwalk assignment took us to the top of the Hyatt Hotel, forty stories high. With San Diego spread before us, we prayed boldly for the peace of the city.

Shortly before the convention convened, I was delighted to meet Carolyn Sundseth when she visited San Diego to attend a women's prayer meeting.[1] This dynamic lady, now in her seventies, had been the

Christian Coalition liaison to the White House during the Reagan administration. With the generous support of Jane Crane from San Diego, she successfully organized an army of several thousand pastors and intercessors across the United States to pray for both the Democratic and Republican conventions.

Carolyn wanted to prayerwalk the convention center, so I took her down and showed her around. Neither of us had tickets to the convention so we prayed that some tickets would become available. By the first day of the convention, we had received tickets for seats in the guest area. We were able to prayerwalk together throughout the day. Later, we found more strategically located seats, higher up, on opposite sides of the auditorium, from which we could cover the area in prayer. I found it difficult to stay focused on prayer in such a stimulating environment, but I prayed that truth and righteousness would be established—yes, even in a political convention.

Carolyn introduced me to many people she had gotten to know during her years in the White House. When she told them we were praying for the convention, all of them reacted positively. I had several opportunities to ask Christian politicians how we could pray for them. The response was always the same, "Strength." I could see the weariness in the faces of these warriors.

Christian delegates told stories of how God had intervened in their lives to get them to the convention and of some of the amazing battles they were facing. We encouraged each other. I was humbled that God allowed me to meet leaders and delegates and to spend so much time with this delightful lady. The city remained peaceful throughout the week, and everyone complimented the police department on how well they handled the convention.

A few days after the convention ended, a picture in the local paper caught my eye. A local group of pagans—polytheists who worship false gods—were pictured coming down one of the staircases where our team had so recently prayerwalked. They were burning sage to purify or rid it of a spirit. I smiled and thought that it was not the GOP spirit they were trying to exorcise, but the Holy Spirit. The following article accompanied the picture.

Center receives cleansing, GOP spirit exorcised

About 75 people made a pilgrimage last night to the now security-free San Diego Convention Center. They were there to perform a spiritual ritual with decidedly political overtones.

"We'll know our mission is accomplished when the gray cloud lifts from the Convention Center," reported the leader. She had organized a cleansing ceremony featuring chanting, drumming, rhythmic movement, and the burning of sage. In no way was this activity intended by its participants to be street theater or performance art. One of those who showed up described the event as "cleansing the convention center of the energy of control."

After about a half hour of sage burning accompanied by thumping drums, rattling gourd and even a soft, ringing sound as someone rubbed a Tibetan bowl, they began the procession around the convention center. The noisy, upbeat crowd augmented the percussion with occasional whoops and yelps as they wound their way through a narrow passageway, stepped carefully over debris from the torn-apart sets constructed for the Convention, marched along the marina and, finally, strolled past a mound of discarded wire and cable the size and shape of a Volkswagen Beetle. All the while, a sympathetic breeze sent swirls of silver smoke wafting toward the sail-adorned building.[2]

This article was further confirmation that we had offered the right prayers for the event. God had indeed been present at the convention. Evidence of that was the retention of the pro-life plank in the platform that year, which is always a battle.

As much as I disagree with their way of thinking, I must say that I appreciated the spiritual sensitivity of the pagans, who recognized that a spiritual battle had been raging while many of our precious Christian brothers and sisters were unaware. I felt as Paul did when he addressed the pagans in Athens who sincerely worshiped many gods. "I see that you are religious. I walked around and observed your objects of worship" (Acts 17:22–23 paraphrased). I prayed with compassion for the day when they would come to know Jesus.

Using the Newspaper As a Prayer Newsletter

How will I know what to pray about? That's a question beginning prayerwalkers often ask. God directs our attention to matters that need prayer in a variety of ways. One of the simplest ways to find clues for spiritual needs is to read the newspaper. News reporters diligently scour the community to find out what's happening. Their findings are presented in the newspaper, on television, and on the radio every day. News reports can be a rich source of information about the spiritual life of your community.

Read and Listen

Read the newspaper as a prayer newsletter, looking for places or events that need onsite prayer. Often, news articles provide key information about why the site is of strategic importance and even include maps or addresses. Pray for your city based on news headlines, key phrases, statistics, charts, graphs, maps, images, or pictures with captions. All of these can stimulate prayer.

Watch and listen to media resources for cross-confirmation of what you sense. The newspaper, television, Internet, and other media identify not only people or issues that need prayer, but places or events that need the informed intercession of prayerwalking. Prayer groups are often the most informed people about what is really happening in their community, both physically and spiritually.

Political leaders especially need our prayer, as we regularly see in the news. Also, more and more Christians are putting their faith into action by seeking political office. As intercessors, we want to pray for all leaders, and pray especially for the success of Christian officials. The newspaper can be your guide in praying for elected officials.

Cindy Jacobs encourages people to "use output from media as matters of intercession. Many prayer groups are now praying extensively for the media that God will raise up righteous reporting of the news in our land. It has often been said that the newspaper is the Christian's report card. By reading the local news we can tell what kind of job we are doing as intercessors."[3]

Pray the News

Ask God to open the eyes of your understanding as you read the newspaper. It's not uncommon for God to point my attention to one or two items in a single day. There are other times when I'll go for several days without reading "prayerworthy" items. Sometimes I notice an article, but do not feel prompted to pray until a week or two later, when a second article provides more information. I find that God was just getting my attention the first time. The second time, I was to pray about it.

Pay attention to those news items that create a quickening in your spirit or create concern. Expect God to reveal information that might lead to a prayer assignment. Be on the lookout for strategic information within the article that will help you target your prayers more effectively. This practice may sound burdensome, but it is not. God spaces out assignments so you don't feel overwhelmed by the needs.

Remember that God likes to use ordinary people for extraordinary assignments. Zechariah 4:10 says, "For who has despised the day of small things?" Job 8:7 also reassures that, "Though your beginning was small, Yet your latter end would increase abundantly."

Keep your eyes open, and you will begin receiving prayer assignments as you read and listen to the news.

Let the News Fuel Your Passion

What do you do when an article or story stirs up your emotions? Use it for the Kingdom by letting God turn your emotion into passion. Turn frustration into action by asking God, "What shall I pray?" Turn fear into boldness by praying strong, active prayers. Turn anxiety into peace by making requests or declarations based on the Word of God.

Pray for intercessors to rise up in hotspots, areas where conflict is taking place. Following the general election of 2000, the nation's attention was focused on Florida, where a recount of the votes would determine our next President. I wondered if there were any intercessors in the Palm Beach area. Were they doing anything? I soon learned there was a team of faithful prayerwalkers praying over the very sites I was watching on television day after day. I added my prayers to theirs.

When crises occur, I no longer wonder if someone is praying. I know there are intercessors all over the country. So I pray that God will stir up intercession, people who will "strive to lay hold of" God (Isa. 64:7 NIV). Haggai 1:14 says, "So the LORD stirred up the spirit . . . of all the remnant of the people; and they came and worked on the house of the LORD of hosts, their God." I ask God to give strength, courage, and boldness to intercessors. I hope others will return the favor and pray for me when the need arises.

Pray on Demand

Some news events such as school shootings, tragedies, or natural disasters, require immediate infusions of prayer. Immediate prayer is also vital for live interviews and talk shows on television or radio. If a Christian is being interviewed by Larry King, I pray aloud before they answer the question, "Speak through them, Lord." If I hear Christians seeming to be defeated in a live interview, I shoot prayers of "Boldness! Boldness!" at the radio or television on their behalf.

When praying for live news events, prepare ahead of time by finding the key Scriptures you will use. I have prayed for "truth and righteousness to be established" in many circumstances, such as during a political crisis. This habit has stood me in good stead because, while I pray it for others, God is establishing it in me as well. I desire it in myself as well as in the other individual or situation.

Truth shall spring out of the earth, And righteousness shall look down from heaven. Yes, the LORD will give what is good; And our land will yield its increase. Righteousness will go before Him, And shall make His footsteps our pathway (Ps. 85:11–13).

Look for Evidence of Spiritual Activity

Both God's work and the enemy's are reported in the newspaper. Recently, the San Diego newspaper gave such a demonstration of God's activity. On Saturday, April 27, 2002, a National Day of Prayer event was held outdoors in front of the historic San Diego County Administration Center on Harbor Drive. Harbor Drive had not been closed off to automobile traffic since President Reagan visited in the 1980s. This area is a showpiece for San Diego, so prayerwalkers were eager to start praying as soon as the street became available at 4:00 A.M. Undaunted by early morning rain, they prayed continuously until the event started at 9:30 that morning. Three thousand Christians of various ethnic backgrounds humbly worshiped and prayed for our nation, state, and county. San Diego is home to more than a dozen military facilities, and our intercession for the military was heightened dramatically when a sailor led us in prayer against the majestic back-drop of aircraft carriers moored across the harbor.

God was pleased, but it was the next day that the headlines revealed what had really happened. No, the story was not on the front page, and, no, it was not about the National Day of Prayer event. The Home Section of the Sunday *San Diego Union-Tribune* featured a beautiful half-page color picture of the County Administration Center. One-and-a-half-inch letters declared accurately "Grounds for Celebration." The article was actually about a new waterfront park being planned for the area where we prayerwalked, but we knew much more was being celebrated in the heavenlies. This was just a sign.

Identify Enemy Tactics

When the enemy encroaches on a community, he brags about it. Early on, I learned the enemy is proud of what he is doing and will expose himself using individuals or events. He does that to put fear and intimidation into the body of Christ so we feel that the situation is hopeless. He hopes we won't try to resist or that we will just give up.

When you read bad news—evidence of the enemy's activity in your community—pray. Counter his strategies by praying boldly for truth and righteousness to be established. You need to be mindful of God's timing, too. Occasionally, you may need to wait until you sense in your spirit, "Now." Then pray with boldness.

Praying the news broadens our compassion, extending it to people we hadn't previously cared about or even known. Fear is removed. We begin to be filled with boldness as we sense the heart of the Father in the situation or for the lost. We pray for the redemption of the very people who oppose us.

We turn adversity to adventure by praying the news!

PRAYER ACTION LIST
How to Use Media to Focus Your Prayer

❏ Pray for your city based on newspaper headlines, key phrases, statistics, charts, graphs, maps, images, or pictures with captions.

❏ Watch and listen to media resources for cross-confirmation of what you sense.

❏ Ask God to open the eyes of your understanding of His work—and the enemy's.

❏ Pay attention to any item that causes a quickening in your spirit or creates concern and expect God to reveal a prayer assignment.

❏ Pray for intercessors to rise up in a hotspot, an area where news is happening.

❏ Look for evidence of spiritual activity in news reports and pray against the schemes of the enemy when you see them.

❏ Prepare to "pray on demand" by identifying Scriptures and prayer strategies that you will use to pray for live media events.

PRAYER FOCUS
Praying the Newspaper

For Speaking and Writing

Isaiah 51:16a: "And I have put My words in your mouth."

Lord, put Your words into the mouths of the reporters, even if they don't know You.

Isaiah 55:11: "So shall My word be that goes forth from My mouth; It shall not return to Me void, But it shall accomplish what I please, And it shall prosper in the thing for which I sent it."

Bless the communication talent You have given to the newspaper staff. Speak through Christian writers and newspapers.

Psalm 56:5: "All day they twist my words; All their thoughts are against me for evil."

Father, we ask You to deal with those who twist the words of truth.

For the City

Romans 16:19b–20 (NIV): "I want you to be wise about what is good, and innocent about what is evil. The God of peace will soon crush Satan under your feet."

You, Father, want to bless this city. Cause us to be wise about what is good. Show us the needs. Cause our steps of obedience to crush Satan.

For Understanding What to Do

1 Chronicles 12:32b: "The sons of Issachar who had understanding of the times, to know what Israel ought to do."

We ask for supernatural wisdom and understanding of the times so that we will know what to do. We pray that Christian leaders will be interviewed for a biblical response to news events, as well as in times of crisis.

Isaiah 52:7 (Amp) "How beautiful . . . are the feet of him . . . who publishes peace."

We pray that Christian leaders will be quoted accurately and be presented in a positive light.

Many nations . . . joined to the Lord in that day . . . shall become My people. And I will dwell in your midst.
—Zechariah 2:11

CHAPTER FIVE

The Sisters I Never Knew

Discovering Unity at Interfaith Prayer Fellowship

Prayerwalk Challenge

Pray with Christians from other denominations

Prayerwalker Skill

Form teams that unite races, genders, and generations

I n the spring of 1997, I was sitting at a luncheon table with approximately thirty women prayer leaders from San Diego when I heard a Macedonian-like call. "Come over . . . and help us" (Acts 16:9). That call was spoken by a lovely African-American woman who urgently invited us to join her for one of the monthly prayer meetings. I didn't catch the name of the group or the location, but I recognized in her invitation an invitation from God. After the meeting, I asked for more information, and before I knew it, I had agreed to attend.

The Interfaith Prayer Fellowship includes representatives from about forty African-American congregations. Some seventy women, a few men, and several pastors meet ten times each year, rotating the location of the meeting among the various churches in the fellowship. Sister Martha Featherston founded the fellowship in 1983 to give African-American women an opportunity to sing, speak, and pray. Few outside that community had heard of the meeting when I began attending fourteen years later.

> After every meeting I looked her in the eye and asked, "Why am I here?"

When I went for the first time, I didn't know much about African-American churches. I felt awkward, out of place, and very self-conscious. I had attended church all my life, so I was amazed at my discomfort in this new setting. For some reason, I felt frightened to walk into the church alone. It sounds foolish, but I'm being honest. As I stood in the parking lot, working up my courage to go inside, something wonderful happened. I met a gracious lady who invited me to sit with her. I nodded with relief. The service had already started, so we sat on the back row where I had a chance to observe and take it all in.

People were friendly, and by the third meeting I felt a strong pull to intercede for these churches. I sensed God was pleased every time I attended, although I didn't know what I was to do or why I was there. The next month, I returned "one more time." I did the same thing the month after that, and the month after that. Each time, Sister Martha wrapped me in love. After every meeting I looked her in the eye and asked, "Why am I here?"

She would laugh, shake her head, and answer, "I don't know."

"It's God, isn't it?" I'd say, and we would stand there holding hands, basking in His presence. I liked being in her presence, too.

For three years I got to know this group by fellowshipping with them in the Spirit, and I kept asking God what I was to learn. From my perspective, the fellowship would have been enough reason to be there. I also enjoyed their joyous celebration and singing. I admired the many soloists who would start singing a cappella. By the third word, the accompanist would catch up with them. Powerful passionate voices!

But the purpose was more than fellowship; God gave me several instructions. The first was that I was to support African-American intercessory leaders. That was easy. It was a real joy to support Sister Martha and the others I'd met.

The next instruction was to intercede for African-American churches. Each time I entered the fellowship meeting I heard the word *focus.* "Focus on what?" I would ask Him. His response was that I was to focus on interceding with His heart for the African-American churches, to see them become connected to the body of Christ—particularly the prayer movement—in order to fulfill their purpose and destiny. I did not know exactly what that meant.

Sister Martha works with her twin sister in the Mamie Leonard Shut-In Ministry. In time, I had an opportunity to share the concept of prayerwalking with Sister Mamie, and she now incorporates prayerwalking into each ministry event. Her ministry is nationally known among African-American Christians. A feature of this ministry is that people are "shut in" to a church for three days of consecration services, where much cleansing takes place. After this preparation, they prayerwalk the church and surrounding area.[1]

In 1999, I heard God say, "Prayerwalk." Since they were already in the habit of covering each meeting with prayer for fifteen minutes at the beginning, it was simple to add prayerwalking at the same time. The first day I prayerwalked there, an eighty-year-old prayer warrior volunteered to be my partner, and we held hands as we circled the church. Unlike former situations, God did not allow me to teach about prayerwalking or make up prayer focus sheets, as I often do. The enemy never had a chance to give the false impression that I was trying to change things.

In 1999, I heard God say, "Prayerwalk."

A few of us continued to prayerwalk each month. Usually my husband, Martha's husband, Brother Ken Featherston, and at least one person from the host church would join our small team. We concentrated our prayer on the hosting church and its community. The police have San Diego divided into neighborhoods based on community lines. They had produced a map with the names of the neighborhoods printed on them. God directed us to call the neighborhood by its name as we prayed.

I sensed God directing me especially to pray Ps. 89:1–23 (especially verses 2, 4, 13, and 14). For three years I prayed it over each church where we met, asking for truth, righteousness, and justice to be established more fully, and for increased discernment. Sometimes we focused more on needs of the people in the particular area, and at other times we focused our prayers on the unseen spiritual battles in the area.

Once, while prayerwalking by a church near the trolley station, I heard myself declaring, "Expose the enemy."

"What is this about, God?" I asked.

Within a week, one of my friends, an African-American intercessor who is on the city housing commission, said she had just learned of a tunnel where gang members were hanging out and causing trouble. She wanted a team to go prayerwalk the area.

A week later, we gathered a multiethnic, multigenerational team of five men and five women including African-Americans, Hispanics, and Caucasians. An apartment complex manager directed us to a large, graffiti-covered tunnel nearby. She joined us in praying for and anointing the area. She had been trying to rid the area of malicious activity and greatly appreciated our support.

One team member, a Hispanic youth leader, had lived in the area as a young man. He explained to us the significance of the competing gang graffiti, and we coached him about what to pray on site. Even as a first time prayerwalker, he had more authority in the Spirit to pray for his own generation than we did. He prayed for the youth to have a sense of belonging to the Father. Before we left, we buried our Scripture-filled prayer focus sheets under a rock near the entrance.

Within days after praying to "expose the enemy," God had directed our attention to His target, put together a team, and used it to help police and other agencies restore peace to a church and neighborhood.

Forming Teams That Unite

Multiethnic teams are urgently needed, and God is using these teams to build relationships and create a breakthrough. I was motivated to get involved in multiethnic prayer ministry, in part, by John Dawson's book, *Healing America's Wounds*. In it, he makes a compelling argument that the Caucasian church in America will not survive unless it repents, is reconciled to, and honors Christian brothers and sisters of other races, particularly Native American and African-American.

Richard Twiss, a Lakota Sioux, states that "Christ's Church will not be truly restored until [reconciliation] happens among the peoples who originally inhabited the land where God had placed them"[2] Jay Swallow, a Cheyenne Sioux leader from Oklahoma says, "Our Native American leaders not only want to be included in what God is doing in this season but are willing to take their place of authority and responsibility to see America turn back to God."[3] This is humbling.

I'll be honest and admit that I was partly motivated by self-preservation as I got involved with multiethnic teams. But there were other reasons. I have a tender heart towards God and I'm quick to obey. I asked God, "Why did you pick me to go to the Interfaith Prayer Fellowship meetings?"

God's response was, "You like family reunions, don't you?" It's true.

I honor the many fine Native American, Hispanic, and African-American people of prayer I've gotten to know, both pastors and intercessors. They have taught me much. Reconciliation is a slow process and cannot be rushed. God is at work, however, and the church will begin to experience the fruit of this reconciliation.

Here are some ways to create prayer teams that reach across ethnic, generational, and denominational lines.

Purpose-Driven Teams

"Does God want you to be a part of this prayerwalk?" God has taught me to pose that question to prospective prayerwalkers. This takes away any sense of manipulation and allows the person to sense God in his or her spirit. Remember, if God is in this, He is already talking to people.

Help people to understand the purpose of the group. Prayerwalks are often spontaneous and informal with a different mix of people based on the occasion. Take a few minutes before each prayerwalk to review the purpose. The more people understand, the freer they are to pray. On some occasions, in order to understand God's purpose, we meet together to pray two to three times before prayerwalking.

Multiethnic Teams

One of the most effective ways to pray is with a multiethnic team. The team itself may be a prophetic act or symbol, representing by its very nature the reconciliation that the team itself seeks. The symbolism of specific team members praying together expresses in microcosm the unity and blessing desired for the larger region. The greater the degree to which the team reflects the makeup of the area or topic to be prayerwalked, the more effective it will be. Contact prospective team members who represent the focus of your prayer. Sometimes God will direct you toward specific team members or provide exactly the members you need.

It may seem challenging to assemble a multiethnic team, but it pleases God when His children pray together. We get to know one another in the fellowship of the Spirit, and even if our styles of praying are different, praying together honors one another and symbolizes our humility. Ask humble questions in order to understand your brothers and sisters better. When I have a question for team members who are different from me, I usually explain, "I do not want to offend, but I need to ask a sensitive question. Is that OK?" Then I preface my question by saying, "Help me to understand. Why do you say or do such and such?" People are usually happy to explain themselves and tell their stories. Do not follow their answer with an explanation about yourself. Stay respectfully focused on them.

When a multiethnic team is needed, I believe we need representatives of various nationalities. In our melting pot society, people have interesting heritages, so ask if there is anyone who might stand in for a particular nationality to signify the whole body of Christ. Although few Christian Native Americans are available for prayer teams, it's amazing how many people have some Native American heritage.

The question of lineage has become more common in the prayer community as we embrace both our identity and our redemptive purpose—God's long-term plan for His creation. We want all people to come to the saving knowledge of Christ, so we include as many ethnic groups as possible in our prayer teams.[4]

Mixed-Gender Teams

Prayer teams that include both men and women can be highly effective as long as basic precautions are observed. You can become close to those with whom you spend time praying. Don't give the enemy opportunity by being careless about how people pair up. A good rule is to have men walk together and women walk together. If teams must include both genders, send at least three people.

Married Couples Teams

Give married couples the option to pray as a team. At first I was hesitant to pair married couples because I didn't want them to feel awkward or distracted. I found that couples usually enjoyed praying together and seemed to prefer praying as a team. Instead of facing additional attacks by the enemy during the week, they reported that God blessed them with greater marital unity.

Multigenerational Teams

Unity in the Spirit is a prophetic symbol to break the isolation and the cultural divide that exists among the generations in the secular world. When prayer teams pray for young people, it's wise to include young people on the team. When prayer teams are composed solely of young people, unity can be expressed by asking intercessors, parents, or teachers to provide prayer cover as they walk.

Nadine, an intercessor from Skyline Church, timidly tried prayerwalking with her teenage son, Chuck. She invited him to join her in praying for his high school by prayerwalking together on the school's running track. She didn't want him to feel any pressure so she proposed it as an experiment. Walkers and joggers were commonly seen on the track, so their presence would attract little attention. Chuck agreed. Afterward, he reported, "I really felt God's presence, Mom." This was the first of their many prayer times for that high school.

Many children are learning how to prayerwalk, and it's easy for them to practice by praying for their churches and schools. I encourage children to worship or sing worship songs when they prayerwalk. God is raising up a generation that has the opportunity to learn a great deal about prayer. Author Gwen Sherrer tells the story of prayerwalking with her grandchildren.

To the ordinary observer I am pulling my grandchildren in a little red wagon through a three-block area in our neighborhood. But in reality we are on a prayerwalk.

As we go down the sidewalk, we'll sing, sometimes making up verses to go with popular tunes they already know. Often all we do is sing "Hallelujah" in front of each home. I may offer a short prayer and they add their "Amen." They are learning that prayer can take place outside our home or church and that we really care for neighbors.[5]

Special Team Members

When creating a team for a special purpose, remember that team size is not what's important. The right mix is. The team may include a *resource person*, someone with knowledge of the subject or area of prayer concentration. When we prayerwalked the tunnel where gang activity had been taking place, we invited the apartment manager to join us, and she even prayed with us. Let the resource person know his or her information is vital to the effectiveness of the team, and create an atmosphere of acceptance, even if that person doesn't feel adequate to pray "like you do." Explain that we each have a role and that his or her contribution is needed for this prayer effort.

Also try to include symbolic representatives who have positional authority. For example, try to include a member of the church, organization, or business that is the focus of a prayerwalk. Include someone who resides or owns property in the targeted area. This is especially helpful when praying over the land. These symbolic representatives may carry more authority into an area to which they belong than you would. If you can't find someone who has positional authority, stand in the gap for those places by continuing to walk in increasing earned authority.

When you work together to form new relationships and create strong, united teams, God will begin to reveal new strategies to revive and transform your community.

PRAYER ACTION LIST
How to Join with Others in Prayer

❑ Determine the purpose of your prayer effort.

❑ Decide who will be invited based on the purpose of the group.

❑ Recruit team members by asking, "Does God want you to be a part of this prayerwalk?"

❑ Try to include a resource person or team member with positional authority for the area you are prayerwalking.

❑ Clearly communicate the purpose of the group to members.

❑ Communicate with people who are different from you in a non-threatening way.

❑ Be open to what God will say to you through the experience.

PRAYER FOCUS
Teams that Unite

For Oneness with Him

Isaiah 2:2b–3: ". . . The mountain of the Lord's house shall be established. . . . And all nations shall flow to it . . . He will teach us His ways And we shall walk in His paths."

Father, cause us to flow toward You.

Ezekiel 37:22a: ". . . I will make them one nation in the land . . ."

We pray for the unity of believers. Many nations (ethnic groups) are represented in our cities, and therefore in our churches.

John 17:21: "that they all may be one, as You, Father, are in Me, and I in You; that they also may be one in Us, that the world may believe that You sent Me."

Lord, make us one that You may be recognized and honored.

Ezekiel 37:6–7: "I will cause breath to enter ... are the bones came together, bone to bone."

We ask You God, to do what Ezekiel asked so the bones would come together. Breathe on us. We are like spokes of a wheel, the closer we are to You, the closer we are together.

For Establishing God's Presence

Zechariah 2:5, 11: "'For I,' says the Lord, 'will be a wall of fire all around her, and I will be the glory in her midst. . . . Many nations shall be joined to the Lord in that day, and they shall become My people. And I will dwell in your midst. . . .'"

Establish a wall of fire around this church property as protection. We invite You to dwell in our midst and in the midst of this church.

Psalm 89:14: "Righteousness and justice are the foundation of Your throne; mercy and truth go before Your face.

We pray for an increased hunger to know God and an increased desire for righteousness and justice. We ask You to establish Your throne among us that we may live in the light of Your countenance.

"For I," says the Lord, "will be a wall of fire all around her, and I will be the glory in her midst."

—Zechariah 2:5

CHAPTER SIX

The Church That Bought a Fire Truck

Praying for Protective Agencies

Prayerwalk Challenge

Pray for a protective agency

Prayerwalker Skill

Pray in emergency situations

Our church was in the middle of a building project that had taken far longer than anyone expected. There were lots of unforeseen problems, and after fifteen long years, the church still lacked one required signature to secure a building permit. The fire chief refused to sign. He was withholding his approval of the project until his department received the promise of a "voluntary" $60,000 contribution with an initial payment of $12,000.

Our pastor and several men had an appointment with the chief and the department's board of directors to present the church's point of view. The chief had seen an opportunity to gain partial funding for a new fire truck, and he had been unwilling to adjust the fee in previous meetings. The congregation was asked to pray.

Our intercessory prayer team had met several times to pray about this issue, and we felt that on site prayer was needed. A team of four people, including me, slowly prayerwalked the perimeter of the fire station's corner property before and during the meeting.

> Our assignment was to pray for protection from the very people who protect us.

We found it ironic that our assignment was to pray for protection from the very people who are supposed to protect us. Although we believed that they were causing a hardship to the church by their unreasonable requirements, we offered prayer for their blessing and protection. We prayed in the spirit of Ps. 5:11–12, "Father, we take refuge in You and are glad. Our hearts are singing for joy as You spread Your protection over our church, the pastor, and the men as they make their plea, and over the fire chief and board, and the people who work out of this fire station. Spread Your protection over this community."

We declared, "In Your Word, You say that You bless the righteous. Our church is trying to go about this in a righteous, just, and fair way. You are surrounding us with Your favor as with a shield. You are giving the church representatives wisdom, knowledge, and understanding as they speak and deliberate. A good plan will preserve us and allow our new church building to open on time."

Then we petitioned the Lord, "Cause the pastor to have favor with God and man as he speaks (Luke 2:52). You, our Redeemer, are strong; the Lord of hosts is your name; You shall thoroughly plead our cause, and give rest to our land" (Jer. 50:33–35). We enjoyed reminding the Lord that He said, "For the oppression of the poor, for the sighing of the needy (and we were sighing!), now will I arise. . . . I will set him in safety for which he yearns" (Ps. 12:5).

We had prayed for God's help and protection and declared His Word. When we felt that our work was finished, we went home.

Unfortunately, the pastor's plea that night fell on deaf ears; the fire chief would not change his mind. At the end of the meeting, the pastor handed the chief a check for the initial fee. In a moment of humor, the pastor asked, "So, when do I get to see my fire truck?" The group laughed and proceeded to the garage to see the new ladder truck. Our delegation returned home feeling defeated because of the meeting's result.

The following year the pastor invited firefighters to bring the ladder truck to the lighting ceremony for the church's forty-foot Christmas tree. Two thousand people were gathered around the tree, set on a hill near the church, visible from the nearby highway. As the ladder was slowly extended to the top of the tree, the choir sang the "Hallelujah Chorus." A fireman climbed the ladder, then slowly reached out his hand to the tree as the lights burst on. This act of reconciliation helped to restore the relationship between the fire department and the church.

The Christmas tree was covered with brilliant white lights, and I privately nicknamed it "The Burning Bush." The burning bush in Exodus was a sign of God's presence. Moses heard God's voice calling to him from the burning bush, and Moses called it a great sight. God told Moses to take off his shoes because he was on holy ground. It was there that God revealed to Moses His name, I Am, and sent him to deliver the children of Israel from captivity.

Our "burning bush" touched our hearts every time we saw it. We had received our own deliverance, not because we had avoided paying the fee, but because we were able to pay it with a spirit of forgiveness. Our church had not only opened on time, but we were now celebrating our first Christmas. The "burning bush" Christmas tree of December 2000 reminded us of God's faithfulness.

Praying for the Protection of Those Who Protect You

Who are the people who protect your community? Probably you could name a number of people who serve in volunteer or government agencies that benefit your community: police, firefighters, ambulance crews, the military, medical workers.

It is not always possible to pray on site for these people because their headquarters or workstations are not always accessible. And when they are dealing with emergencies, it is impossible to prayerwalk on location. When you do pray on site at a police station, fire house, or other facility, be careful that you do not disturb the work that is taking place. One way to pray on location is to prayerwalk around the outside of buildings or on the public sidewalks in front of police headquarters or fire stations. You might be able to prayer-walk the perimeter of the property or circle the block where the headquarters is located. You can also pray standing on a high place that overlooks a facility such as a military installation. Branches of the military have many storefront recruiting offices, which can be targets of a prayerwalk. They also provide visible reminders to pray for our servicemen and women. Military personnel and civil employees of the military may be able to actually pray on site at military bases.

  Whether you can prayerwalk for protective agencies or not, you can still pray for their safety and protection. Here are some ways to pray for the protection of those who protect you.

Use Flare Prayers When You Can't Prayerwalk

  Because I can't always prayerwalk easily around protective agencies, I've learned to stop and pray only if God points out a specific site to me. Most often, I use *flare prayers* while driving around the area.

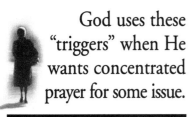

God uses these "triggers" when He wants concentrated prayer for some issue.

Flare prayers are short, targeted prayers. A flare prayer may be triggered by something visual, such as the sight of a police car or fire truck. A wailing siren or accident report on the radio can also trigger the need to pray.

  I believe that God uses these "triggers" as prompts when He wants concentrated prayer for some issue. When I'm at work, busy with the tasks of the day, I may never think to pray for law enforcement. But when I'm driving and catch sight of a police car, God may use that visual cue to remind me to pray for the police. When God prompts you to pray by means of these reminders, send up a flare prayer for the blessing and protection of those who are racing to the scene of an emergency.

Target Prayers on the Needs of the Agency

  When I see or hear of a police officer heading into an emergency situation, I pray for supernatural wisdom. An officer in the field has to make instant decisions. San Diego Homicide Officer Mequel Penulosa explains, "People need to understand the difficulty in police work.

When you are on patrol or are an investigator, you are the one that confronts the criminal."[1]

When driving by a police headquarters or county sheriff's office, pray for the administrators who work there. They must allocate resources to best meet the needs of the community. Pray for supernatural wisdom so that they will use resources wisely. Also pray for the proper training of the officers and for the wisdom of the leaders in dealing with the political situation in the city or county. Pray that the administrator will be able to set wise priorities.

Law enforcement is a high stress occupation. Sadly, those who deal with life-and-death situations are often affected by them—some even commit suicide. As you pray, speak life into them and their families. Psalm 5:11–12 says, "But let all those rejoice who put their trust in You; Let them ever shout for joy, because You defend them; Let those also who love Your name Be joyful in You. For You, O LORD, will bless the righteous; With favor You will surround him as with a shield."

God often uses traumatic experiences to draw people toward Him. Pray that those who deal with sickness, crime, and tragedy every day will be drawn to the Lord because of what they see. Pray that they will call upon Jesus and develop a relationship with Him.

Pray also for the spiritual sensitivity of emergency personnel. I heard a policeman report that due to the extreme stress that they face, particularly since the tragedy of 9-11, one of their greatest problems has been lost sensitivity, especially toward their own families. Many officers rely on alcohol to cope. Domestic violence is a common problem.

Pray for the peace and healing of their wounded souls. Pray that they would seek comfort through the Holy Spirit, rather than through alcohol. Pray also for the families of emergency workers. They make many sacrifices in lifestyle so that we may be protected.

Pray for God's Will to Be Done

The enemy is at work in our world, including in your community. His work needs to be exposed. We do that not by focusing on evil but by focusing on God. God has sent the Holy Spirit to teach us as well as comfort us. Listen for the voice of the Holy Spirit so that you'll know when to pray and what to pray about. Pray for all the people that protect us, whether they know God or not, that they will have the ability to discern good from evil in every situation and to do their jobs well.

Pray for the development of stronger connections between the spiritual leaders of your community and the protective agencies that serve it. Pray that Christians in these protective agencies will grow stronger in the Lord and have favor in their work. Pray that these departments will be blessed, that any corruption be exposed. And pray for redemption to come to those who have been weak or led astray. Pray for good judgement. Pray for justice to be done. Also pray that they will seek wise counsel and that the agencies that protect us will sense that the Body of Christ supports them with prayer.

As I see police cars going by, my first reaction is to check my speedometer. My next response is to pray that the Lord will check the police officer's speed. I pray, "Lord, give them supernatural wisdom and discernment even if they don't know You. Protect them and those they apprehend. Cause the officers to know that You are their friend and want to help them in their work."

Cover Emergency Situations with Prayer

Late one night my friend Glenda Pettit and I were returning home from a prayer meeting in Dallas. We were traveling westbound on Route 121 toward her home in Euless, chatting away as usual. When we came into Irving, we met a wall of red taillights, meaning that traffic was clogged ahead. Glenda launched into an avalanche of prayer for protection over the accident ahead. I looked sideways at her and wondered, "How does she know there is an accident?" I was tired and felt no compulsion to pray. Still not sure that there even was an accident, I just let her do it all. A few minutes later, we slowly passed two eastbound cars on the shoulder of the road and several police cars with red lights swirling.

Later that night, the phone was ringing as I entered my home in Bedford. My mother called to ask if I'd heard about my niece Janie's car accident. I responded, "Oh, no! Don't tell me it was on Route 121!" Sure enough, Glenda had just prayed for our pastor's daughter and my niece. Fortunately, the police had responded quickly and she was not hurt.

Since that memorable night, whenever traffic begins to slow I immediately pray for protection for everyone involved in the situation, including the officers. I pray not only for their physical well being, but that they will come to know God better through the accident. Finally, I pray for the financial well being of those involved. Every accident is inconvenient and costs something. The effect can be devastating financially.

With police emergency lights flashing, fire sirens blaring, and troops constantly poised for war, we need to be ready to pray for emergencies at any moment. These Scriptures can be used to cover emergency situations with prayer.

- That evil will be exposed, Eph. 5:13 (NLT): "But when the light shines on them, it becomes clear how evil these things are."
- That evil will be cut down, Matt. 3:10: "And even now the ax is laid to the root of the trees. Therefore every tree which does not bear good fruit is cut down. . . ."
- For protection, Ps. 91:3–4: "Surely He shall deliver you from the snare of the fowler And from the perilous pestilence. He shall cover you with His feathers, And under His wings you shall take refuge; His truth shall be your shield and buckler."

Psalm 91 may be personalized to pray for a specific person or protective agency. When prayed in this way, it becomes more of a declaration—a statement of our faith. To personalize this Scripture, insert the name of the individual or agency for which you are praying. I carry these verses in my car and when I need a Scripture prompt, I pull it out. I've highlighted a few words to trigger my memory.

Psalm 91

_____ who dwells in the secret place of the Most High Shall abide under the shadow of the Almighty. _____ will say of the LORD, "He is my refuge and my fortress; My God, in Him I will trust" (vv. 1, 2).

Surely He shall deliver _____ from the snare of the fowler And from the perilous pestilence. He shall cover _____ with His feathers, And under His wings _____ shall take refuge; His truth shall be _____'s shield and buckler (a small shield) (vv. 3, 4).

Because _____ has made the LORD, who is his/her refuge, Even the Most High, his/her dwelling place, No evil shall befall _____, Nor shall any plague come near his/her dwelling; For

He shall give His angels charge over _____, to keep him/her in all his/her ways. In their hands they shall bear _____ up, lest he/she dash his/her foot against a stone (vv. 9–12).

"Because _____ has set his/her love upon Me, therefore I will deliver him/her; I will set him/her on high, because he/she has known My name. _____ shall call upon Me, and I will answer him/her; I will be with _____ in trouble: I will deliver him/her and honor him/her" (vv. 14–15).

PRAYER ACTION LIST
How to Pray for Protective Agencies

❑ Allow the Holy Spirit to prompt you to use flare prayers.

❑ Pray for protection and wisdom for those responding to emergencies.

❑ Pray for the peace and protection of the community.

❑ Pray that emergency workers will be shielded from the stress of their work and that their families will be blessed.

❑ Pray that the enemy's work will be exposed and that God's will shall be done.

❑ Pray that those who lead protective agencies will have discernment to see what is good and evil in every situation.

❑ Pray that corruption will be exposed.

❑ Cover emergency situations with prayer.

PRAYER FOCUS
Protective Agencies

For Protection

Psalm 5:11–12: "But let all those rejoice who put their trust in You; Let them ever shout for joy, because You defend them; Let those also who love Your name Be joyful in You. For You, O Lord, will bless the righteous; With favor You will surround him as with a shield."

Father, we ask for Your protection.

Psalm 34:7: "The angel of the Lord encamps all around those who fear Him, And delivers them."

We are asking the Lord of hosts to send forth angels to encamp around us and this situation.

Psalm 35:4b: "Let those be turned back and brought to confusion Who plot my hurt."

Bring confusion to the enemy's plans.

1 Corinthians 4:5b: ". . . who will both bring to light the hidden things of darkness and reveal the counsels of the hearts."

Lord, we ask You to expose the schemes of the enemy and any hidden thing.

For Unbelievers

2 Corinthians 4:4 "Whose minds the god of this age has blinded, who do not believe, lest the light of the gospel of the glory of Christ, who is the image of God, should shine on them."

Father, we come against any mind-blinding spirits. Rip off the veil, unveiling the truth.

For Believers

Ephesians 1:17–18: "[May] the God of our Lord Jesus Christ, the Father of glory . . . give to you the spirit of wisdom and revelation in the knowledge of Him, the eyes of your understanding being enlightened. . . ."

Open the eyes of our understanding.

For Blessing

Psalm 43:3: "Oh, send out Your light and Your truth! Let them lead me; Let them bring me to Your holy hill and to Your tabernacle."

Bless them Father, with light and truth. Bless them with whatever they do not have but need.

Plans are established by counsel;
By wise counsel wage war.
— Proverbs 20:18

CHAPTER SEVEN

Announcing God's Plans on Television

The 1996 Presidential Debate

Prayerwalk Challenge

Prayerwalk a nationally televised event

Prayerwalker Skill

See God's strategy as it unfolds

In the fall of 1996, San Diego hosted one of three televised debates between President Bill Clinton and his Republican challenger, Bob Dole. This debate was to be held on the lovely campus of the University of San Diego, a Catholic university. The campus, with its neat rows of white, Spanish-style buildings, sits atop a lush, landscaped bluff overlooking the San Diego harbor and the Pacific Ocean. The school is home to Immaculata Cathedral, a beautiful building located at the center of the campus.

The debate would take place in Shiley Theatre, a small building capable of holding only about two hundred people. In honor of the occasion, the theatre had undergone an expensive makeover. A stage was created to accommodate two podiums for the debaters and places for the moderator and camera crews. Seats surrounding the stage were reserved for common people who would ask the questions.

Because a presidential election is a tremendously important event in the life of our country, we felt that it was important to prayerwalk the debate if at all possible. Several intercessors made advance visits to the campus to research the area. They noticed clues to the school's original purpose from the symbols and plaques that dotted the campus, and they observed its current spiritual flavor from the many posters and signs scattered about. They discovered that the theatre was just two buildings away from the cathedral.

Later, we learned that the area would be secured on Monday, two days in advance of the Tuesday evening debate, which would be watched by millions of television viewers. Starting on Monday morning, only those with passes could get on campus, so we decided to prayerwalk the debate area on Sunday afternoon.

Our team gathered by a fountain at the center of the campus. The team was quite diverse, including both men and women, and people of several races, including Filipino, African-American, Caucasian, and Native American. We had a number of older people and one college student, Ted. We divided ourselves into teams of two or three to prayerwalk designated areas of the campus and arranged a time to reassemble for group prayer near the Shiley Theatre.

> Because any presidential election is tremendously important, it was important to prayerwalk the debate if possible.

It seemed that the only people on campus were members of the national news media and a few construction workers. When we stumbled onto a side door of the theater, several of us decided to step in and pray briefly. We didn't want to interfere with what the workers were doing, and we wanted to maintain the freedom to move about the campus, so we dispersed around a courtyard in the center of the building. I encouraged our team to be discreet. We prayed together, enjoying the quiet and serene atmosphere.

As I prayerwalked quietly around the perimeter of the courtyard, I noticed a number of large windows that opened onto the courtyard itself. I could see some journalists who sat at desks facing the windows. We had been praying for awhile when suddenly, I looked up and saw, to my horror, a television newscaster holding a microphone to Ted's face. He was being interviewed! A young man about Ted's age balanced a camera on his shoulder while the young reporter interviewed Ted. Ted looked relaxed and calm, but I wasn't!

God used the cameraman to broadcast a prayer appeal to the city.

"Oh, no!" I thought, "They think they are talking to a local student but Ted isn't even from this school. If they find out we're here praying, they might suspect that we're up to something and ask us to leave."

I quietly motioned for the others to follow me out the front door to the outside of the building. Ted was the last to come out to join us. We surrounded him as he told the story. He was praying silently when the reporter approached him and began the interview.

"What are you doing here?" the journalist asked. "Are you studying?"

"No," Ted explained, "I am praying for the debate and for peace and safety on the campus." This seemed reasonable to the interviewer because there had been reports of possible protests which were added to the usual concern for the safety of the candidates. The young man thanked Ted and told him that he was filming the activity on campus.

That night on the six o'clock news, the pre-debate report included the segment with Ted, praying for the peace of the campus. I wondered if the university president was watching and trying to remember if he had ever met this serious student. Although he was enrolled at another college, his comments sounded entirely appropriate for a religious university.

This was the first prayerwalk for most members of our team, including Ted. Yet within one hour of arriving on campus, God picked the only college student on the team to announce to San Diego, via the evening newscast, that this momentous event would be blanketed in prayer. God used the cameraman's need for an interesting story to broadcast an appeal to the city to pray. We wanted our presence on the campus to be hidden. God wanted it to be revealed, and He did it by using a most ordinary, humble person. The more experienced members of the team were amazed to see God's strategy unfold.

God was at work in other ways. At church that Sunday morning, I mentioned to my friend, Barbara, that we were going to prayerwalk near Shiley Theater that day. She mentioned a Scripture from the Psalms that she felt God had given her for Bob Dole the day before. She interpreted this to mean that if he would stand for righteousness, God would bless him. At the last minute I had written it into the prayer focus sheet that we would use at the university.

Several days after the prayerwalk, I shared that story with my sister-in-law, Carol Garlow. Soon afterward, she and her husband, Jim, were invited with a group of local pastors to attend a prayer breakfast for Bob Dole. Since Pastor Jim was to give the invocation, he and Carol were seated at the head table. During the benediction, Bob Dole's wife, Elizabeth Dole, got up and stood behind Carol until the prayer was finished in order to slip out quickly. Carol turned to Elizabeth Dole and said, "This scripture is for your husband," giving her the verse. Elizabeth asked her to repeat the reference and thanked her.

I was stunned at how fast God had worked. First, Barbara, who does not see herself as an intercessor, had sat in her home having devotions and felt God speak to her. Then, within a few short days, the words God had given her were spoken almost literally, into the ear of one of the most powerful people in the country. We don't know what the results of that may have been, but we felt sure that God had used our faithfulness as a part of His unfolding plan.

Watching God's Strategy Unfold

A strategy is a plan or series of maneuvers designed to produce a desired result. The military uses a strategy to ensure security or produce victory. God has a strategy in mind for us when we prayerwalk. Sometimes we understand the entire plan at the outset, and at other times, as in the case of the presidential debate, we see it unfold during the event. Often, we do not know the significance of what God has asked us to do until much later. It is fascinating to follow Him.

In March of 2001 we saw another example of God's strategy unfolding. A student at Santana High School in Santee, California, shot and killed two classmates at school. My husband and I felt prompted to attend a community prayer service in Santee the following day. We arrived early at the site of the prayer service and found the parking lot nearly empty. We decided to stand outside and face in the direction of the school (although we could not see it) and pray for both the school and the city of Santee. We had our eyes open and were taking turns praying quietly out loud.

Out of the corner of my eye, I noticed someone approaching us. I turned to see a television reporter walking toward me. A satellite truck had parked in the far corner of the parking lot. The reporter asked if we would come closer so that he could interview us.

"I'll ask you why you are here," he said.

We nodded in agreement, and I thought about what to say as we walked over to him. Immediately, I felt that God wanted me to communicate two simple sentences. I rehearsed them out loud with my husband, hoping I could remember them under the spotlight. I decided no matter what question he asked, I would answer with my sentences. God's strategy, I believed, was to stir up prayer and to let the people of Santee know they were being supported in prayer.

The reporter asked Keat the first question, then he directed a question to me. I have no idea what it was; I just answered with my two sentences: "We are from La Mesa and we have come to support the school and the city of Santee in prayer. Many people from around the area are praying for Santee."

I felt anointed as I spoke, assured that my words would call others to prayer. The sentences were simple, obvious statements, yet I felt that the Holy Spirit had communicated through them. The reporter smiled and thanked us. Forty minutes later, there were more than a thousand people in the church auditorium. I found myself wondering if anyone had watched that television station, since we did not. Just then, a woman seated in front of us turned and said, "We just saw you on TV."

Later, I saw a pastor come in late and go straight to the front. Afterward he told us, "When I saw you on TV, I thought, 'I'd better get down there.'"

That was the confirmation I needed. God had stirred His people. We didn't know that would happen when we set out for Santee. We simply watched His plan unfold and played the part that He had directed us to play.

When God unfolds His strategy before our eyes it causes us to have more trust in Him. He exposes areas of unbelief we did not even know we had, and we begin to have more confidence in our ability to follow. We respond with less delay, confusion has no place to rest, and despair evaporates. You may not always know what God's strategy is when you set out for a prayerwalk, but you can see it happening and take part. Here's how to catch a glimpse of what God is doing.

Be Alert to Unusual Happenings

Note unusual happenings, conversations, or connections that seem to have an element of divine leading. An example of an unusual happening was noted by an intercessor when she read in the newspaper that a light post had fallen over, killing two people in downtown Fort Worth, Texas. The article stated that that area was known as Hell's Half Acre. She thought at first, "Surely someone must already be praying in that area." Later, she realized the incident was her call to prayer. God used the report to get her attention, and she took action.

After you have prayed for a particular area, keep informed about breaking news concerning that place. Talk with people who might have some connection to the issue. Ask, "Have you noticed anything lately related to—?" Look for evidence of God's plan unfolding even after you have done your work.

Sense God's Strategy through Worship

Worship can move us past our own mental barriers to get in tune with the Holy Spirit. As Chuck Pierce and Rebecca Wagner Sytsema have said, "If you come into a new place of intimacy and communion with God, your eyes will be opened to see new strategies that break the enemy's power."[1]

Worship takes us to a level where we can hear God speaking more clearly. Psalm 25:14 says, "The secret of the LORD is with those who fear Him, And He will show them His covenant." Someone has said that the word *secret* in this context means guidance from the Lord. When we worship God, He reveals things to us. What an awesome privilege to be trusted with the secrets of God!

There are some times, however, when we are unable to see all that God has planned. I believe He lets us peek at His strategy sometimes in order to extend an invitation to draw even nearer to Him. He tries to whet our appetite. Paul talks about hidden wisdom being revealed. Strategies come to us from this hidden wisdom.

But we speak the wisdom of God in a mystery, the hidden

wisdom which God ordained before the ages for our glory . . . But as it is written: "Eye has not seen, nor ear heard, Nor have entered into the heart of man The things which God has prepared for those who love Him." But God has revealed them to us through His Spirit. For the Spirit searches all things, yes, the deep things of God (1 Cor. 2:7, 9–10).

I find that worshiping on my own often starts out dry for the first few minutes or longer. At this point worship is truly a sacrifice of praise. But after a time, it's possible to break through to a place where joy and faith are released. If we press on in worship, the Lord will take us to a higher place. There, He may use Scripture or songs to impress or alert us about some aspect of His strategy. When that happens, we must descend from the mountaintop moment to carry out what He has said. God has released a new strategy from the throne room.

We cannot pray very long or very many times without exhausting our human abilities. When we find that we are running on empty, we have to go back to the Father to be renewed with the Word and through worship. In fact, we have learned that if we begin to lose energy as we are prayerwalking, we should start worshiping as we walk. Sometimes God uses that time to shift gears, revealing a new strategy to the team. And when we worship, we are renewed like the eagles (Isa. 40:31).

Worship is key to understanding God's strategy. By drawing close to Him we can become instruments of righteousness to carry out His will on the earth. That is why spending time in worship or being in a spirit of worship helps us to respond rapidly to carry out His will. It could be that you are the one to whom God will entrust a mission. It may be you who He wants to use to get the ear of the mayor, politician, businessman, or other decision maker.

PRAYER ACTION LIST
How to Recognize God's Strategy

❑ Worship God wholeheartedly, and be attentive for what He might choose to reveal about His strategy.

❑ If you sense that God is calling you to a task while worshiping, act upon that prompting.

❑ Be alert to unusual happenings, conversations, or connections that seem to have an element of divine leading.

❑ Go prayerwalking even if you have little or no strategy and watch how He unfolds His purpose for you.

❑ Be sensitive to God's leading during prayerwalking, using occasional times of worship to allow God to refresh you.

❑ Stay current on news concerning your prayer site so that you may see God's strategy unfold after you have prayed.

PRAYER FOCUS
Worship to Refresh

Songs of Revelation

Revelation 4:11: "You are worthy, O Lord, To receive glory and honor and power, For You created all things, And by Your will they exist and were created."

Father, our heart sings this song to You.

Revelation 5:12: "Worthy is the Lamb who was slain To receive power and riches and wisdom, And strength and honor and glory and blessing!"

Father, You are worthy to receive power, riches, wisdom, strength, honor, glory, and blessing.

The Priesthood of Believers

1 Peter 2:4–5a: "Coming to Him as to a living stone, rejected indeed by men, but chosen by God and precious, you also, as living stones, are being built up a spiritual house, a holy priesthood. . . ."

We thank You for making us living stones—a part of the kingdom of God that You are building.

1 Peter 2:9: "But you are a chosen generation, a royal priesthood, a holy nation, His own special people, that you may proclaim the praises of Him who called you out of darkness into His marvelous light."

We come to You today as a royal priest. We praise You for calling us out of darkness.

Hebrews 13:15: "Therefore by Him let us continually offer the sacrifice of praise to God, that is, the fruit of our lips, giving thanks to His name."

We offer You the sacrifice of praise. We give thanks to Your name.

Behold, how good and how pleasant it is
For brethren to dwell together in unity!
—Psalm 133:1–3

CHAPTER EIGHT

The Power of Joining Hands

A Day of Prayer at Sacred Heart Chapel

Prayerwalk Challenge

Pray in a multidenominational setting

Prayerwalker Skill

Tap into the power of agreement

I had never done anything like this before! I first experienced Tapestry, a prayer ministry for women,[1] at a prayer event held at Cathedral Church of St. Paul in San Diego. When it was time for voluntary prayer and singing, our voices floated throughout the beautiful Episcopal sanctuary as if we were a large choir. A year later, on October 2, 1999, Tapestry held another day of prayer for women from southern California in the Chapel of Loyola Marymount University in Los Angeles.

Bonnie Shannonhouse, the founder of Tapestry, believes that God has called her to unite women with one another to acknowledge the holiness of God, to hear God's Word, and to offer prayer and corporate worship in the cathedrals of the world. She was calling for a consecrated fast (see Joel 1), with women from all denominations gathering in cathedrals for individual and corporate prayer and for instruction in the disciplines of daily prayer. As Bonnie likes to say, "Tapestry weaves a beautifully corded picture of God's people."

> **We needed to show unity by forming a multiethnic team.**

When we gathered in Los Angeles we received instruction from Bonnie as well as Joy Dawson, the mother of John Dawson who heads the International Reconciliation Coalition. Joy said that it had been one of her dreams to speak to Catholic women. That made this occasion, held on the campus of a Catholic university, a gratifying experience.

Prior to the event, we were reminded to be considerate of the chapel, our hosts, and their traditions. We were free to prayerwalk inside the chapel unless services were in progress. I facilitated prayer and prayerwalking before the big day as well as on the Day of Prayer. As a San Diego resident, I sensed a particular urgency to capitalize on opportunities for San Diego to support and cooperate with Los Angeles. Both vast metropolitan areas can become complacent about the physical and spiritual needs of other regions. I felt that we needed to come in the opposite spirit and show unity by forming a multiethnic prayerwalk team with members from both cities.

Several prayerwalks had been conducted around the chapel area and throughout the campus. On Saturday morning, before the start of the Day of Prayer, our team stood outside the chapel. I sensed in my spirit that we should lock arms and march once around the building. God even gave me a picture of how we were to stand. Our group comprised Filipinos, Hispanics, Caucasians, and Pacific Islanders.

The six of us locked arms and walked around the chapel, praying audibly. At one point, we even broke into song. Locking arms was a prophetic act that visibly demonstrated our unity in the Spirit. God blesses when brothers dwell together in unity. Marie was on the outside of the line. She is very sensitive to the Holy Spirit and described feeling a cold and awful presence that went away as we continued. I felt that God was pleased by this representation of the Body of Christ.

That was not the only expression of unity on that day; we were part of something truly groundbreaking. Later, several young prayer-walkers who were former Catholics reported feeling great discomfort at being back in a Catholic church. When they realized that they harbored unforgiveness in their hearts towards the Catholic Church they repented and received God's forgiveness. One woman in particular returned to her family with a much different attitude. After repenting of her own critical spirit, God brought about a restored relationship with her parents. It truly is a wonderful thing when God's people dwell together in unity.

Tapping into the Power of Agreement

The power of agreement comes from agreeing with God's will. Matthew 18:19 is a foundational verse for understanding the prayer of agreement. "Again I say to you that if two of you agree on earth concerning anything that they ask, it will be done for them by My Father in heaven." We, as believers, do not randomly pick things on which to agree. We must first come into agreement with the Word of God. We line up our thoughts and our desires with what God wants (Isa. 55:9). Agreement is a powerful prayer tool. The word itself is derived from a Greek word that means *harmony* or *symphony*. When we agree with God, we're taking part in a grand symphony of which He is the conductor.[2] Terry Teykl writes that "agreement is covenant language, and it is powerful. . . . it means we have the power to act on earth in accordance with our God in heaven with whom we are 'bonded.'"[3]

Here are some practical steps for tapping into the power of agreement in your prayers.

Seek the Mind of God

The first step to praying in agreement is to seek the mind of God. Since it is Him with whom we must agree, it makes sense that we should learn God's plan and bring ourselves into agreement with it. Seek the mind of God through prayer. Study His Word to understand what He thinks and what He is doing in the world. No prayer can truly be in agreement with God unless it agrees with what He has already said in His Word.

Affirm the Prayers of Others

Praying in agreement can be compared to filling a water bottle. One person puts a little water in and another adds more water. The process continues until the bottle is filled. Never underestimate the importance of one prayer. We never know who else has prayed or is praying. That's why our prayers matter for future generations. We are praying in agreement with those who will follow us, maybe even our own descendents.

Find out what has been prayed previously in a location and see what you can come into agreement with. You may be only the latest of a large number of people to pray fervently for something. As you prayerwalk in the footsteps of previous intercessors, bear in mind that you "are surrounded by so great a cloud of witnesses" (Heb. 12:1). These are they who have completed their races, passing the baton to us, and cheering us on as we complete our leg of the race. The Living Bible calls them "a huge crowd of witnesses to the life of faith."

Agree on the Purpose of a Prayerwalk

Agreement about the purpose of the prayerwalk should permeate every aspect of preparation. This starts with agreeing on a clearly stated objective, the more specific and measurable the better. Christians often pray in a shotgun fashion and then wonder why they don't see results. Our prayers should be more like a guided missile— aimed at a specific target. It's up to the prayerwalk leader to help the team focus on the prayer agenda for that walk. Once God's assignment has been clearly identified, team members should be allowed the freedom to pray for that assignment in their own way.

Sometimes, I sense that God has revealed to me the number of people that are needed to agree together to achieve a breakthrough in a certain situation. I invite that number of people to join the prayerwalk. At other times, I don't have that clear sense about the number of people to invite, so I simply begin with a group and allow God to reveal more specifics if He chooses.

Evaluate the Target

When selecting a team of prayerwalkers, consider what kind of *stronghold* you are dealing with. A stronghold is a fortified place that Satan uses to oppose the work of God.[4] Paul wrote, "For the weapons of our warfare are not carnal but mighty in God for pulling down strongholds" (2 Cor. 10:4). The more strongly entrenched the evil that you are opposing, the more prayer that will be required to break it down.

Before that can happen, it's important to break down our own, personal strongholds. One writer described a personal stronghold as "a mind-set impregnated with hopelessness that causes the believer to accept as unchangeable something that he or she knows is contrary to the will of God."[5] When believers accept these footholds for the enemy in their lives, the result is hopelessness and disabled faith.

Evaluate the Team

When looking to tap into the power of agreement in prayer, it's important also to evaluate the spiritual maturity of the team members. Veteran prayer warriors usually have dealt with their own strongholds and are able to pray more effectively. Generally, we recognize the spiritual maturity—hence, the spiritual authority—of believers by the fruit of the Spirit in their lives (see Gal. 5) or the results of their prayers.

Fast

Prayer and fasting linked together bring us into greater agreement with God's purpose. We increase the effectiveness of our prayers by fasting. Fasting makes us more sensitive to the Spirit of Truth. Another way to express agreement is by fasting together as a team on the day of the prayerwalk.

Cultivate a Spirit of Unity

When developing a prayerwalk team that has not prayed together before, it's good to have the team pray together several times before taking on a big project. That way, team members can be free to pray together in whatever manner feels most comfortable. This helps people to get to know one another and makes it easier to come into agreement with God's purpose for them. Each team member should have an opportunity to contribute, and the leader can provide necessary direction.

Psalm 133 describes the beauty of brotherly love and how good it is when people dwell together in unity. It compares unity to oil upon the head. In Old Testament times, a fragrant oil was used in the ritual of consecration for high priest (Exod. 29:7). Unity is also compared to the dew of Mount Hermon. Mount Hermon was known for unusually heavy dew, which was a great blessing in an arid country. God's blessing and healing gravitate to the fragrant oil and fruitful serenity of Christians living in unity.

Of course, unity is not achieved in an instant. Some teams struggle to come to agreement. If a team member urges prayer for something contrary to the team's prayer goals, suggest another option and look for areas of common ground. Use the opportunity to explain the importance of agreeing in prayer.

When you are invited to prayerwalk with someone, it's important to agree on the goal. The prayerwalk leader may pursue a goal that is not well defined or violates Scripture. When I receive invitations to prayerwalk, I usually ask, "What do you want to happen here?" That question helps to clarify the goal.

Learn to Agree Even When You Disagree

It is quite possible to pray effectively with Christians who hold different views than we do if we focus on the need at hand without getting sidetracked. Ted Haggard says, "When we pray to raise the level of the Holy Spirit's activity in our city, many times we end up praying for ministries that interpret some portions of Scripture differently from the way we interpret them or have a different culture from ours. But they are still life giving. Therefore we must view our differences as a strength, which means appreciating one another's respected interpretations of Scripture."[6]

You can learn to pray in agreement, even with those with whom you disagree on important matters.

Persist in Prayer

When you prayerwalk in agreement with God's purpose and with other believers, be persistent in prayer. When God alerts you to pray and you feel a great urgency, knowing that others are praying with that same sense of urgency, it means that you are nearing a breakthrough. Yours might be the final prayer that God uses to break the resistance to His will.[7] Keep praying.

There are several types of prayers that can accomplish a breakthrough. One is called *supplication*. Supplication is like pleading with God in a life or death situation. You may sense the need to enter into supplication for a specific site and prayerwalk there. You may never know the result of your prayer, since it may avert some action that would otherwise have taken place.

Travail is another type of prayer. The word *travail* can mean to experience birth pangs. It is a God-given desire to pray intensely, sometimes loudly. Paul used this term in Gal. 4:19 (KJV), speaking of his prayer on behalf of the church in Galatia. "I travail in birth . . . until Christ be formed in you." I have travailed for my children as well as for other situations, as have many intercessors. Sometimes we can only groan, as Paul says in Rom. 8:26–27:

> Likewise the Spirit also helps in our weaknesses. For we do not know what we should pray for as we ought, but the Spirit Himself makes intercession for us with groanings which cannot be uttered. Now He who searches the hearts knows what the mind of the Spirit is, because He makes intercession for the saints according to the will of God.

Travailing is not something to be done on a prayerwalk in a public place. However, when you feel a deep prayer burden, as Jesus did in the Garden of Gethsemane, you should quickly go to a place where you can freely pour out your heart before God. The length of time it takes to travail may be rather short or quite long. Be prepared to persist in prayer until it is done. When the travail is finished, you will feel a release in your spirit. You may sense that that episode of travail was simply one stage in the process of praying for a particular burden, or you may sense that the process has been completed.

Don't be afraid of intense emotions as God stirs your heart for your family, church, community, or your nation. However, since this is such a strenuous spiritual activity, it's wise to educate the intercessors in your circles so they can pray along with those who are in travail and share the burden.

Expect a Breakthrough

One cloudy day Patricia and I sensed the presence of a "great cloud of witnesses" when we prayed together at the base of a sixty-foot cross atop the mountain on which our church is built. We enjoyed the beautiful San Diego weather as we prayed that day, participants in a countywide prayer event held at various strategic sites. Patricia and

I read several Scriptures aloud and then knelt before the cross to spend time adoring the Father. We felt humbled as we knelt, appreciating the opportunity to stand in the gap for many people. We thanked God for the many prayers that had been prayed in agreement with His will from that very spot. We sensed that witnesses were cheering us on, encouraging us to keep going and bring about a breakthrough that had been only a dream in their lifetime.

Sometimes God confirms His approval with a sign in the sky, as He did dramatically for Noah by providing a rainbow after the Flood. As Patricia and I stood up and walked to the left of the cross, I lifted my camera to take a picture and realized I was witnessing a spectacular moment. A shaft of sunlight had broken through a hole in the clouds to illuminate only the heart of the cross—the point where the crossbars intersect. I gasped, "Look Patricia!" We stood speechless, amazed at the confirming sign that God had provided. He had sealed this day. We felt blessed, and felt that we had been joined in this time of consecration by the many who had gone before us, never seeing the fulfillment of their dream of a new church built on that property.

PRAYER ACTION LIST
How to Pray in Agreement

❑ Prayerfully seek the mind of God to confirm that you are in agreement with Him.

❑ Find out what has been prayed there before concerning the issue, and see how you might pray in agreement with it.

❑ Deal with your own spiritual strongholds, breaking down any personal areas of resistance to God's will.

❑ Evaluate your target to determine the number of people to invite to pray.

❑ Evaluate the spiritual authority of your team to be sure that they are ready for this prayer challenge.

❑ Build a spirit of unity by clearly defining your goal, praying together, and fasting together.

❑ Cultivate unity by focusing on praying for the need at hand, not debating the points on which you might disagree.

❑ Be persistent in prayer, expressing yourself freely in supplication or travail as God directs you.

❑ Expect God to break through in answer to your prayer.

PRAYER FOCUS
Prayer in Agreement

Preparation

Matthew 18:19: "Again I say to you that if two of you agree on earth concerning anything that they ask, it will be done for them by My Father in heaven."

We pray these verses over our team (or myself) like warm oil. Let them permeate our minds.

Ephesians 4:1–3: "I, therefore, the prisoner of the Lord, beseech you to walk worthy of the calling with which you were called, with all lowliness and gentleness, with longsuffering, bearing with one another in love, endeavoring to keep the unity of the Spirit in the bond of peace."

Enable us to keep the unity of the Spirit through humility, gentleness, longsuffering, and love.

Uniting Ourselves with Him

Psalm 86:11: "Teach me Your way, O Lord; I will walk in Your truth; Unite my heart to fear Your name."

Teach us Your ways that we may unite ourselves with You.

Amos 3:3: "Can two walk together, unless they are agreed?"

Show us how You want us to walk together with You.

"Strengthen the weak hands, And make firm the feeble knees. Say to those who are fearful-hearted, 'Be strong, do not fear! Behold, your God. . . .'"

—Isaiah 35:3–4

CHAPTER NINE

Marching in the Shadow of Man

Overcoming Fear in Balboa Park

Prayerwalk Challenge

Pray in a public parade

Prayerwalker Skill

Overcome fear

On a Saturday morning in June of 2000, we assembled in a grassy area of Balboa Park near Sixth and Laurel Streets for the latest San Diego March for Jesus. The route we would follow took a curving road to the south, then circled around a large flagpole where there was a lovely view of the city skyline. From there it headed back north to Laurel Street and then east across the Laurel Street Bridge, famous for its beautiful archway over Highway 163. At the end of the bridge, the route crossed under an archway and passed through a short canyon of buildings.

At one point, the route passed the rising spires of the Museum of Man. This museum was built for the 1915 Panama-California Exposition and immediately became a signature landmark for San Diego. The Panama Canal had just opened, and San Diego was trying to compete with Los Angeles to become a major port. The 1915 Exposition was so successful that it remained open two years. San Diego did attract the U.S. Navy because the San Diego Harbor was ideal and the climate couldn't be more perfect; the temperature remains around seventy-two degrees year round. The Pacific Fleet is based here and controls the seas for much of the world.

From the Museum of Man, the march took us past several blocks of buildings, ornately built in the style of Spanish colonial architecture, that originally were intended to be only temporary additions to the 1915 Exposition. Turning south just past the Museum of History, the route faced the beautiful Spreckel Organ Pavilion. John D. Spreckel built the outdoor Organ Pavilion with the stipulation the organ would be played at 2:00 P.M. every Sunday afternoon, and so every Sunday there is an organ recital. The metal benches can seat two thousand people. The front of the Pavilion is probably three stories high, and the organ and its pipes are housed inside. The organ is pulled out on stage for concerts.

What I love about the Organ Pavilion is the arcade that encircles half the Pavilion on either side of the open-air stage. Cool breezes blow through the arches and you can see tree branches waving in the breeze. The twenty arches of the arcade form spectacular picture frames. Every time I go there I imagine each archway festooned with huge colored flags waving in harmony as a packed Pavilion fills the air with worship.

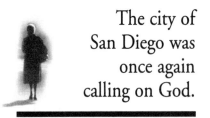

The city of San Diego was once again calling on God.

Balboa Park has a rich religious history. In the 1920s, Aimee Semple McPherson held healing revivals at the park, drawing crowds of thirty thousand people. The city fathers and church leaders of that era turned out to hear her speak. Photographs of her praying for people in the Organ Pavilion can be found in history books of the city. As we gathered for the March for Jesus, I was reminded that the city of San Diego was once again calling on God.

Lining up for the march in a grassy area, we knew that the worship band was playing onstage at the Organ Pavilion. It was totally quiet where we were assembled, however, about a mile away. We had planned to march in silence until we rounded the corner toward the Pavilion. We had brought shofars, which are ram's horns similar to those used by priests to call people to prayer in Bible times. A shofar was blown to signal the start of the march.

> As we began to cross the bridge, the walk suddenly seemed foolish to me.

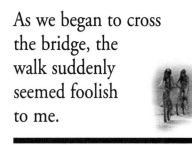

Then, all we could hear after that was the shuffling of our feet.

Many people carried colored flags. A friend had loaned a white flag to me. The white stood for holiness. I had never carried a flag in a parade before, but I was pleased to carry this one because of my heritage in a holiness denomination. I gently waved the flag back and forth in cleansing waves and began to relax.

Every parade held in San Diego follows this same route, including the Gay Pride Parade, which had been held a few weeks earlier. The police had cordoned the area. Since we marched only on streets that run through the park, we would have very few spectators until we got across the bridge. The trees and police officers stood silently as we marched by.

As we began to cross the bridge, the walk suddenly seemed foolish to me. It seemed as if nothing was going to happen. I felt no anointing. "Why am I doing this?" I wondered. We seemed even more insignificant as we passed by the majestic Museum of Man, which had come to celebrate evolution. Here we were—a tiny group of Christians who appeared impotent shuffling past this imposing, world-famous building. "Who are we," I thought, "compared to this landmark that can be seen even by airline passengers as their planes swoop down to approach Lindbergh Airport?" I had been gripped by fear.

At that moment, it was as if God spoke directly to me, saying, "You are here to honor the Creator!" Faith welled up within me. My arms began to swing the flag in broad, diagonal strokes as if I had broken chains. I felt as if the white flag had become a sword of holiness cutting through the air. I smiled at a small group of Native Americans preparing native food for a celebration that day. My arms did not want to stop, so I confidently slashed my sword and my heart sang. "We've come to set the people free! Deliverance! Freedom!" I prayed for deliverance from deception for all those who worship man instead of the Creator.

As we rounded the corner toward the worship team a half block away, something hit us. It was the heavy weight of God's Glory. The worship team also felt this, only they felt pushed back by that weight as we came toward them. The blowing of twelve shofars kicked off two hours of worship. One shofar blower produced the most incredible sounds. None of us could identify who he was. Maybe he was an angel!

Dealing with Fear

Everyone feels fear. Sooner or later, you, too, will experience fear as you pray or prayerwalk. That's normal. When God created us, He graciously gave to us the capacity to recognize danger and make an immediate, instinctive response. Fear itself is not a bad thing; God uses it as a way to protect us. But God doesn't want us to linger in fear or to become immobilized by it. When we are afraid, we must recognize the fear, identify the source, and deal with it.

Satan is quick to capitalize on our natural fear response and twist it to make us fearful in situations where fear is not warranted at all. He uses fear to undermine our faith in God and make us question His goodness and reliability. We can deal with fear by approaching it in the opposite spirit—faith.

Here are some practical ways to respond when you feel afraid during prayer.

Rely on Faith

We come in the spirit opposite of fear when we exercise faith in God and in His promises. One of the clearest promises we can use to combat fear is found in 2 Tim. 1:7. "For God has not given us a spirit of fear, but of power and of love and of a sound mind." The word *fear* used here means timid or faithless. The word *spirit* means breath or blast. When we are hit with a blast of fear or faithlessness, that fear can immobilize us and make us feel powerless, self-absorbed, and irrational. God can replace this fear with a sound mind, disciplined with self-control. That leads to self-confidence.

It takes practice to learn how to combat fear and to operate in a faith mind-set. We must learn to identify inappropriate fear when it arises, return to a mind-set of faith, and remain there. The first step is to realize that it *is* possible to overcome fear. That enables us to return to a faith outlook quickly instead of feeling paralyzed or helpless in the face of fear.

I once had an interesting conversation with a Navy SEAL, a member of the Navy's elite special warfare unit. I asked him how he dealt with fear, and he told me, "When you are in combat you don't own fear. You give it to God. Concern and fear are different. Concern is biblical, but fear shows a lack of faith. You renounce it. If you freeze up you are already dead. You have to respond and react or you will freeze and die. You cannot be fearful for your life."

We must not own fear either. When we feel afraid, it is an opportunity for God to deal with unbelief in our hearts. Lack of faith leads to a spirit of timidity and loss of hope. When you feel afraid, let your first response be to renew your trust in God. Fear evaporates in a climate of faith.

Pray to Establish God's Will on Earth

In our nation, much ground was given to the enemy in the 1960s and 1970s. We are reaping the results now. Many Christians are trying to take the ground back, but we are not looking backwards. We are looking forward to establish God's will on the earth.

Places like Balboa Park may seem like pleasant places to be, but often there are others who are using those public places for unholy purposes. As we begin to look at our community through God's eyes, it can be frightening to see its true spiritual condition. Yet God will enable us to deal with fear so that we can see His strategy for dealing with the situation.

We might be afraid because of the unknown or because we don't know what to do about a troubling situation. We often feel afraid when we feel helpless. Helplessness is a common source of fear these days, considering how rapidly the world is changing around us. Yet as we get in tune with God's strategy and begin to cooperate with it, God begins to exercise control in what seem like hopeless situations.

One time, Suzanne Burgess, a friend and fellow intercessor, and I were visiting the Museum of Man in Balboa Park when she noticed some words written on the floor of the doorway. "This site dedicated to Truth-Liberty." She seized upon a portion of what was written and began to pray Scripture with those words in them. "Let them [man] know the Spirit of Truth and where the Spirit of the Lord is, there is Liberty for them. Holy Spirit, draw men's hearts to Christ Jesus Who is truth for their life" (John 8:32; 2 Cor 3:17; John 14:17).

Although the enemy has a strong grip on some places, God's power is greater, and His will shall be done on earth.

Use the Power Found in Jesus' Name

There is power in using the name of Jesus. After all, we nearly always pray "in Jesus' name." C. Peter Wagner points out, "The Bible pays careful attention to the power that is embodied in names, especially in the 'Name of God' and in the 'Name of Jesus.' . . . Jesus said, 'And I will do whatever you ask in my name' (John 14:13 NIV). To use the name of a person implies a certain authority granted by that person."[1]

When you feel afraid, use the power found in Jesus' name.

Take Authority in the Spirit

You can avoid becoming timid, especially in public situations, by recognizing the authority that you have in the Spirit. You have the authority to pray in any place where you have a legal right to be. That includes places where you have bought a ticket, like a ballpark or a museum, public places like malls, and private homes where you've been invited socially or on business. You can take authority in your prayer by claiming your right to be there and commanding demonic powers to flee. It's called the *I'm Here, You're Gone* prayer, and it goes something like this:

> O God Most High, I am your servant.
>   I have a legal right to be in this place.
>   I am covered by the blood of Your Son.
> Because of the blood of the Lord Jesus Christ,
>   and the word of my testimony,
>   and my covenant relationship with You,
>   I ask for your protection in this place,
> And I ask that you would cause any forces of the enemy to flee.

I've used this prayer several times in situations in which I felt afraid. Once when I was prayerwalking, I noticed some suspicious things going on in a nearby parked car. I prayed the *I'm Here, You're*

Gone prayer, and within thirty seconds, the car pulled away. As a believer in Christ, you have spiritual authority. When you feel afraid, claim that authority in Jesus' name.

The enemy would love to frustrate your attempts at prayerwalking by causing you to feel timid, powerless, and afraid. There is no question but that you will face fear as you pray and prayerwalk. That fear will be a normal response to new and different situations and to the powers of darkness that you confront by your very presence. Rather than surrender to fear, rely on faith. As Paul rightly observes, "If God is for us, who can be against us?" (Rom. 8:31). There is power in the name of Jesus.

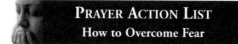

PRAYER ACTION LIST
How to Overcome Fear

❑ Do not be alarmed by the fact of feeling fear; realize that it is a natural response.

❑ Identify your fear and evaluate the source, then approach the situation in the opposite spirit—faith.

❑ Combat fear by trusting in God's promises.

❑ Elevate your faith by praying for the establishment of God's will on earth and specifically in the place where you are.

❑ Use the power found in Jesus' name to claim protection in frightening circumstances.

❑ Take authority in the Spirit by understanding your position when you announce, "I am a child of the Most High God."

PRAYER FOCUS
Taking Authority in Jesus Name

Identity

John 1:12: "But as many as received Him, to them He gave the right to become children of God, to those who believe in His name."

I am a child of the Most High God.

Hebrews 13:20–21 "Now may the God of peace . . . through the blood of the everlasting covenant make you complete in every good work to do His will, working in you what is well pleasing in His sight, through Jesus Christ. . . ."

I am in a covenantal relationship with the God of peace who is making me complete to do His will.

Action

2 Timothy 2:7b: "May the Lord give you understanding in all things."

Lord, You give us understanding in all things.

Revelation 12:11: "And they overcame him by the blood of the Lamb and by the word of their testimony. . . ."

We overcome by the blood of the Lamb and the word of our testimony.

2 Corinthians 6:4, 7: "But in all things we commend ourselves as ministers of God. . . by the word of truth, by the power of God, by the armor of righteousness on the right hand and on the left."

Lord, You clothe us with the armor of righteousness.

2 Corinthians 10:4–5: "For the weapons of our warfare are not carnal but mighty in God . . . bringing every thought into captivity to the obedience of Christ."

I bring every thought captive to Christ.

Romans 13:12: ". . . Let us cast off the works of darkness, and let us put on the armor of light."

I put on the armor of light that dispels the darkness.

Righteousness and justice are the foundation of Your throne; Mercy and truth go before Your face. Blessed are the people who know the joyful sound!

—Psalm 89:14–15

CHAPTER TEN

When God Came Back to the Mountain

Skyline Church Relocation

Prayerwalk Challenge

Pray for a church building project

Prayerwalker Skill

Develop a prayer strategy

When our church's prayerwalk team was first assembled, we began, like many churches do, drawing mostly from beginners. We didn't have many mature intercessors to draw from, as we do when we select a prayer team from an entire city or region. We welcomed anyone who was interested enough to come. We trained a lot of people, but when it came time for a prayerwalk project, many were unavailable because of work or other commitments. Our prayerwalk teams often numbered between twelve to twenty people, which was actually very manageable. We were blessed to have mature intercessors from other churches, who were eager to share their insights and encouragement and help us get going.

In those days, we often faced circumstances that were new or different, and we were learning a great deal. Each prayer meeting and prayerwalk increased our faith that God would reveal a little more of His strategy for our group.

> We often faced circumstances that were new, and we learned a great deal.

One of the things we did was research the history of prayer in San Diego and in our church. We felt that it was important to know the prayers, intercessory or prophetic acts that had been made, and their results. We sought to honor all those who had labored in prayer over the years without seeing the final results. It is always important to preserve a record of what God has said and done so we can remember it for ourselves and pass it along to others.

In time, our prayer team grew in strength and number. We had been having weekly intercessory prayer meetings for three years. Now we were preparing to relocate our church to a mountain seven miles away, having outgrown our current facilities.

The congregation decided to relocate in 1983 and had bought a large tract of land on a mountain in 1988. In April of 1992, a fifty-foot cross was erected on top of the mountain during a dedication service near the site of the proposed sanctuary. Construction was scheduled to begin by 1993, but it was delayed many times by a series of technical problems. In 1998 we planned the long awaited crossing of our "Jordan River;" a groundbreaking service was scheduled for August 30.

One of the problems we had encountered in the relocation was the strict environmental rules governing the use of the new property. The Skyline staff was so concerned about the stringent regulations that they didn't permit us to prayerwalk on the property. They didn't want to risk another delay. It was a tense time for our congregation. I was asked to lead intercessory prayer meetings for each of the four weeks preceding the groundbreaking. Since we couldn't pray on site, we met in the building that was the closest to the new property line. Carol Garlow, the prayer director at our church, and I had a number of

Scriptures that we felt the Lord had given to us, and we asked God to give us a sign we were praying on target.

Honestly, I didn't want to be present at the first meeting. Everyone was frustrated over the delays in the building project, and our troops were just plain tired. I wasn't sure how many people would be there, since we'd made only a general announcement that the building was open for prayer; it wasn't a scheduled service. I always want to be present when God shows up—no matter what. Yet I know that when He does come, it usually costs someone something. It might require some intense intercession, or fasting and prayer, or warring all night. Aside from the Scriptures we'd prepared, I had nothing to offer the team. While driving to the first prayer meeting, I told the Lord, "I'm so spiritually tired, I don't think I could swat a fly. I'm afraid that if You don't do something at this meeting, nothing is going to happen." We had a prayer plan, but we didn't have much energy. We needed God to act.

Over the next several weeks, that's exactly what He did. Here's the story of how God visited our mountain and cleansed the land.

August 4: The Presence of God

On the first Sunday, we prayed for the manifest presence of God (Exod. 33:3–16; Ps. 89:15–29) to be evident and for God's favor to rain down on the pastor, staff, relocation team, construction workers, and the people of Skyline. We declared Ps. 89:22, "The enemy shall not outwit us." We also asked God for a sign to show us that we were praying on target. This was the start of something big, for those August prayer meetings and the accompanying signs were profound and dramatic.

August 10: Fire

The next week, we prayed for a wall of fire and the Glory of the Lord to surround Skyline mountain (Zech. 2:5). The next morning we woke to a spectacular local news report of a roaring inferno creating a towering column of fire from a ruptured gas line—right beside our property. I hollered out loud, "God, Don't burn up the mountain!" The following day, the *San Diego Union-Tribune* ran a photo of the blaze, appropriately captioned "A Pillar of Fire!"

We were amazed and took that as a sign, although horrified by this accident, and asked God to protect our mountain from fire.

August 18: Water

On the third week, we prayed for rivers of living water (Ps. 46:1–5; Eph. 5:26; Ps. 36:8–9; John 7:38–39) to run around and through the mountain property, giving life to the development of the land and the construction of the buildings.

At about the same time, someone noticed an unused underground water line. We were required to build a bridge over it before we could even unload the earthmoving equipment. An empty water pipe on a waterless mountain! While this seemed like an incredible sign to the intercessors—a symbol of the living water that would soon flow—it was not amusing to the pastor or the relocation team. Sometimes, intercessors keep their supernatural revelations to themselves!

It took several weeks to build this "bridge over no water," and the delay prevented the large, earthmoving equipment from entering the land. In the meantime, only lighter vehicles would be allowed on the property. Pastor Garlow had given his word to the congregation that equipment would begin operating on August 17, 1998. He was determined to keep his word, so he asked a staff member who was familiar with construction equipment to go rent bulldozers or anything that moved. In a most manly prophetic act, Pastor Jim got on the caterpillar and *took the land by force.* I recalled Jesus' description of the coming Kingdom, "From the days of John the Baptist until now, the kingdom of heaven has been forcefully advancing, and forceful men lay hold of it" (Matt. 11:12 NIV). We made a small beginning at preparing the site for construction. The dust flew, and we all rejoiced that at last we could legally occupy the land.

August 24: Earth

The final week, we prayed Scriptures about the land (Ezekiel 37:14). While reading Ezek. 36:33, our prayer group felt the purifying fire, and no one moved or said anything for many minutes. Three times I tried reading aloud, "On the day that I will cleanse you of all iniquities," and each time I would say, "On *that* day." I literally could not complete the verse. There was a sense that God was going to do something *in one day.* We all knelt silently on the floor, humbled ourselves before His Holy Presence, and waited for a long while. We sensed that nothing else needed to be said or done, so we closed the prayer time. Yet we knew that God was not finished.

August 30: Wind

Sunday, August 30, was the day of our groundbreaking ceremony. Early that morning, the intercessors went to a high point overlooking the gathered congregation. Suddenly, this Scripture seemed to leap off the page of the prayer focus sheet. "I am the LORD, your Redeemer; I am the Holy One of Israel. You shall be a *new threshing instrument with many sharp teeth. You will tear all your enemies apart,* making chaff of mountains. . . . the wind will blow them all away . . ." (Isa. 41:14–16 NLT, emphasis added). We had skipped over this Scripture all month because it hadn't seemed to make sense before now. I later learned that it was accidentally included in the prayer sheet. God must have hidden it from the proofreader's eyes!

At the conclusion of the service, Pastor Jim Garlow, with the spiritual authority that rests upon him, drove the earthmover up the mountain. When the front blade struck the ground, it seemed to be a divine statement about God's authority over this land. This prophetic act declared strongly that this mountain belongs to God. The watching congregation broke into cheers, and later, many reported that the most important moment of the entire service was when the procession of earthmovers went up the mountain "taking the land" after twelve long years. Two mature believers with the spiritual gift of prophecy later confirmed that they, too, felt the land had been cleansed and that there was a different spirit on the mountain.

God had applied the promises from Zech. 3:9 and 13:2 to us. ". . . I will remove the iniquity of that land in one day. . . . In that day, says the LORD of Hosts . . . I will cut off the names of the idols from the land, and they shall no longer be remembered. I will also cause . . . the unclean spirit to depart from the land." Our prayer times and ground breaking had culminated in the sudden release and cleansing of the land.

Skyline Church held its Relocation Celebration in May 2000. In honor of that occasion, my husband, Keat, wrote this poem commemorating the intercessors' story of what God had done.

Majesty On the Mountain

When all the paperwork is done,
After the technical battles won,
The healing waters shall flow (John 14:4),
And there will be Majesty on the Mountain (Isa. 2:2–3).

The scriptures hidden in the walls (Ps 119:161; Ps 119:25)
Will flow as sparkling water falls (John 7:38–39)
As they continue to speak
From the Majesty on the Mountain.

When the last steel has been set in place,
And the Throne room is given space (Ps 89:4),
The Word of God shall be proclaimed (Ps 107:20)
From the Majesty on the Mountain.

The fire of God shall roar (Zech 2:5),
The healing waters pour (Is 44:3)
O'er the land of restoration from the One (Ps 85:1)
Who inhabits the Majesty on the Mountain.

All God's people shall be blessed
As they enter into His Rest
And worship Him forever
From the Majesty on the Mountain.

The roar of Judah's Lion,
Gentleness from the Lamb of Zion,
The shadow of the Cross of Christ,
Embody . . . the Majesty on the Mountain.

Renewed for the battle for the souls of men
We shall go forth to serve amid the din
In a spirit of sacrificial love
From the Majesty on the Mountain.

Forged by His Presence (Zech. 4:6–7),
Filled by His Essence (Ps. 85:9),
Truth and righteousness will flow (Ps. 89:9; 85:11, 13)
From the Majesty on the Mountain.

Inhabiting the Majesty on the Mountain . . .
He is the Majesty of the Mountain.

—Keat Wade

Learning to Identify God's Prayer Strategy

Praying for your church, its programs, projects, and ministries is one of the most important things you can do. Our churches need to be strong. As Pastor Jim Garlow frequently points out, "The battle will be won or lost in the local church. Not anywhere else."

As you pray for your church, it's important to have a prayer strategy. We know that what we do will mean nothing without God's intervention—we need Him to show up and do something great. Yet God often responds to our carefully determined and faithfully executed plans. Prior to the groundbreaking, we had no energy and little enthusiasm. But we did have a strategy, and we followed it. God chose to honor that faithful effort with a mighty act.

Here's how you can develop a strategy for prayer at your own church or elsewhere.

Seek God

Remember that it is God's will we seek; therefore it is God's strategy that we must find. Before you begin a prayerwalking project, spend time seeking God. Bring your group together for times of prayer and worship. Be open to the moving of the Holy Spirit. Allow God to reveal to you what He wants you to do. Also spend time alone, as individuals, seeking God's strategy for your group. Plans that you conceive on your own will have little effect. If the Lord directs your prayer strategy, you'll be effective in your prayers.

Research

In this book, you've seen a number of prayer strategies employed, with varying results. Our team is constantly fine-tuning its strategies, seeking to find the right approach in each different situation. We make use of experts, like George Otis Jr., who gather research data that track prayer trends worldwide. We can also keep data ourselves to gauge the effectiveness of our prayers. God is constantly teaching us how to pray. Our intent is not to manipulate Him but to align ourselves with His purpose.

We also do research on our area, which often reveals specific spiritual needs that become targets of prayer. During the relocation project, when there was conflict between the congregation and local authorities, we came in the opposite spirit, praying for blessing upon those whom we felt were opposing us. One intercessor blessed the water district by Eph. 3:20, "God can do abundantly far more than we can ask or imagine." He prayed, ""Give them a waterfall of blessings, Lord." Keep current on news about your area.

Agree on Goals

If your team is to function together, the team members must agree on the purpose of the prayerwalk and its goals. Determine what you believe God wants you to do. Agree on the approach you will take, the times you will meet, the places you will go, and the number of meetings you will have. Everyone who joins the effort should know what the plan is and agree to participate in it.

Choose Scriptures to Guide Your Prayer

In praying for our church's relocation, we relied heavily on Scripture. Scripture provides a framework for our prayer and keeps our minds focused.

You may have noticed that I have referred often to Psalm 89. I use this psalm frequently in prayer, and I don't mind repeating it. Psalm 89 shows not only God's might and His character, but also that the covenant He made with David continues to affect us today. While we were praying over the relocation project, God drew my attention to this psalm. My eyes fell on verse 14, "Righteousness and justice are the foundation of Your throne; Mercy and truth go before Your face." We had been praying for truth and righteousness to be established for several years, but I had never noticed it was literally a part of God's throne. At that time, we were all thinking about the actual foundation of the church building, so in my mind's eye I began to picture a gigantic slab of cement which would be not merely a foundation for our church building but also for God's throne. Every time I went near the property, I would pray that God's throne would be established upon the mountain.

Then one day I noticed the word *justice* in that psalm for the first time. Righteousness and justice are the foundation; mercy and truth are the result. Righteousness and justice are the basis of God's rule, and these two words, along with mercy and truth, offer a full description of God's unique character. When I noticed that, I began to pray not only for our church but also for other churches, saying, "I pray for the foundation of righteousness and justice of a church to be established so the throne of God can dwell there." In my mind's eye, I could picture the churches getting stronger as deception fell away from the people and truth was established. So far, I have been praying Psalm 89 for five years, and I am not done yet! When He releases me, I will stop. God has sealed this Scripture on my heart.

Ask the Lord to direct you to the Scriptures that will be effective in your situation. You may find that one Scripture keeps coming back to your mind, or the Lord may give you new Scriptures for each prayer situation. Use them as a guide as you pray. They will become part of your prayer strategy.

Chuck D. Pierce and Rebecca Wagner Sytsema wrote that "the Lord is blowing His Spirit on His Church to make it a new, sharp threshing instrument. . . . He says, 'I need a leadership to demonstrate My purposes on Earth anew. I need an army who will come forth to breakup the enemy's strategies and display My will on Earth. I need government that takes what has been scattered and gathers it together to advance My kingdom.'"[1] We have a right to inquire of the Lord and ask Him to show us overcoming strategy. Let Him give you your verse and overcoming strategy.

PRAYER ACTION LIST
How to Identify a Prayer Strategy

❑ Spend time worshiping and praying in a small group.

❑ Do research on the area, which may reveal the spiritual needs that you will target in prayer.

❑ Pray individually to align yourself with His purposes.

❑ Agree on the goals of your prayerwalk.

❑ Determine the Scriptures that you will use to guide your prayer.

❑ Agree on the specifics of your prayerwalk—when you will go, for how long, and how often.

❑ Continue reading Scripture and praying about your strategy so God can reveal more of His strategy or prompt prophetic acts.

PRAYER FOCUS
Determine a Prayer Strategy

John 10:4, 14: "And when he brings out his own sheep, he goes before them; and the sheep follow him, for they know his voice. . . . I am the good shepherd; and I know My sheep, and am known by My own."

Jesus, we picture You leading us.

Psalm 32:8: "I will instruct you and teach you in the way you should go; I will guide you with My eye."

Let faith arise for You will guide us to gain new strategy.

Psalm 85:12–13: "Yes, the Lord will give what is good; And our land will yield its increase. Righteousness will go before Him, And shall make His footsteps our pathway."

Thank You Father, that You will make Your footsteps our pathway.

Psalm 89:15: "Blessed are the people who know the joyful sound! They walk, O Lord, in the light of Your countenance."

You lead us by the light of Your countenance.

1 Corinthians 2:6, 7, 10: "However, we speak wisdom among those who are mature, yet not the wisdom of this age, not of the rulers of this age, who are coming to nothing. But we speak the wisdom of God in a mystery, the hidden wisdom that God ordained before the ages for our glory. . . . But God has revealed them to us through His Spirit. For the Spirit searches all things, yes, the deep things of God."

Reveal to us Your strategy and guide us by Your Spirit.

With my mouth will I make known Your
faithfulness to all generations. . . .

—Psalm 89:1

CHAPTER ELEVEN

We Walked for Three Hundred Years in One Day

Prayerwalking Old Town San Diego

Prayerwalk Challenge

Pray for a historical site

Prayerwalker Skill

Inform intercession through research

After we had prayerwalked the Caltrans building in the Old Town district of San Diego, we thought that was the end of the story. It wasn't. We eventually prayerwalked every street in Old Town. Old Town is approximately four blocks long and four blocks wide. There are a number of restored historical properties and sites there, including the first capitol of California. Old Town is the site of the first of twenty-one missions established along the California coast. Franciscan missionary Father Junipero Serra built Mission San Diego de Alcala on Presidio Hill in 1769. In 1774, it was relocated to its present location, six miles away, to be closer to a village of Native Americans. The Presidio then became a military outpost, with a stockade and garrison. Old Town continued to grow over the years and became the first center of San Diego.

In 1995, well-known intercessor Steve Hawthorne led a prayer team of forty people, including author and intercessor Lou Engle, to revisit all of Father Serra's missions following the Camino Real Highway (King's Highway, in Spanish) from San Diego to San Francisco.[1] Later, when an archeological excavation temporarily exposed the foundation of the Presidio, our team got inspired and seized the opportunity to prayerwalk this key San Diego location.

Before setting out, I did some research and learned something about the history of this city. Alonzo Horton is considered the founder of San Diego, which was established in 1869. When Horton arrived here in 1867, he found that there was no wharf, meaning that supplies had to be carried in from ships, then loaded on wagons. Horton was the first to see how this area could be developed if a waterfront were added, and the city flourished under his leadership.[2] Over the years, however, Old Town slowly withered as the center of activity shifted. As we researched, the team looked for historical figures that might have had a redemptive contribution to the city's history. One significant man was successful Christian businessman George Marston, who arrived in San Diego in 1870. He was known as an admirable and principled civic leader. He founded the San Diego Historical Society and oversaw the design of the fourteen hundred acres that became Balboa Park. His Victorian house is now a historical site near the park.

> **Before setting out, I learned something about the history of this city.**

In 1907, Marston spearheaded the purchase of the forty-acre property that included the Presidio so that it could be preserved as a park. He was responsible for putting up the adobe Serra Cross at the Presidio. The cross is still there although now people have to hunt to find it. Marston was well regarded because of his tremendous contribution to the city, and he almost became mayor. We felt that Christians could be proud of his contribution and build upon his legacy, especially by reclaiming the parks for God's glory.

Today, Old Town is one of the most popular tourist sites in San Diego. It is connected to the convention center by trolley, and many convention visitors stop by to enjoy the excellent Mexican restaurants. What happens in Old Town affects people from all over the world. As local residents, we might take tourist sites for granted, but they can be of pivotal importance for a citywide prayer strategy.

In addition to reading up on the history of the area, our team interviewed people who knew the area's past, as well as several current business owners in the district. San Diego's fourth grade students routinely visit the historical sites of Old Town, and one of our newest prayer team members happened to be an elementary school teacher. She was a valuable asset because of her familiarity with the area.

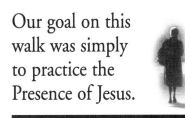

> Our goal on this walk was simply to practice the Presence of Jesus.

After learning as much as we could about the area, we felt that we were ready to prayerwalk Old Town. As we went, we prayed for discernment so that we would know how to pray (1 Cor. 12:10). We asked for wisdom to select the right prayer focus. We didn't pray for everything, but only certain spots as God quickened our spirits. We checked with each other periodically and adjusted our direction accordingly. If we were in agreement on a particular direction, we took it.

Sometimes, timing turns out to be crucial on a prayerwalk. As we follow God's leading, we may find ourselves in places at just the right time. These are called *divine appointments*. On our visit to Old Town, we got to one site where we felt directed to pray just before it was closed.

Our goal on this walk was not to engage in any intensive spiritual warfare but simply to practice the Presence of Jesus. When we found churches in the area, we prayed that the Word of God proclaimed there might bear fruit. We prayed also over historical markers, gleaning what information we could from them and adding our blessing to the good we found. This prayerwalk was enjoyable, if uneventful. When we felt that our task was complete, we went home.

I had asked God why He led us to prayerwalk this area but didn't feel that I had a clear answer. The next week, however, an article appeared in the newspaper, which outlined a political battle that was taking place over the control of Old Town. I looked for more information about the issue, but even after learning more, I did not know what would be the best resolution for the city. I realized that I didn't need to know because God does. It became clear that our prayerwalk was part of a spiritual struggle that I knew nothing about. So I simply continued to pray for the city of San Diego, knowing that His will has been done here in the past—and will be again.

Informing Intercession through Research

I love history and am thankful for the interest of our ancestors in establishing parks and historical sites. By doing this, they showed their respect for the land and for the events that had occurred there. The historical sites of our cities hold valuable clues to guide our larger prayer strategy.

Effective prayerwalkers draw on history primarily to discover the redemptive purpose of an area. George Otis Jr. defines *redemptive purpose* as "a distinct characteristic or facet of every city's life and history that can be seized upon by God to demonstrate divine blessing and truth."[3] For example, a city founded by murderous pirates might have different spiritual needs than one founded by peaceable Quakers. We use research to discover the roots and history of a place in order to bless what is good and redeem what is evil. Here's how research can make your intercession more effective.

Learn the Spiritual History of the Area

Historical sites can be signposts to the spiritual heritage of a place. Identify the important historical sites in your area. Visit one and do a preliminary survey. Pay special attention to the person or event that the site commemorates, the nature and character of those who founded it, the reason that it was established, and its current purpose. Researchers often ask these basic questions about a place:

- What is wrong with my community?
- Where did the problem come from?
- What can be done to change things?[4]

When we studied our historical sites we paid special attention to the motivations and the character of the founders. What did they bring with them, both in the physical and spiritual, that shaped the spiritual character of this community?

Understand the Link between Past and Present

San Diego has many teaching institutions, including universities, hospitals, and cutting-edge research facilities. It is home to more than a dozen megachurches with many gifted teaching pastors. It is also a transportation hub, exporting goods and ideas all over the world. San Diego is a city of firsts: the birthplace of Christianity on the West Coast and home of the first mission in California, where the first Christian martyr in California died in 1775. These are not unimportant facts but valuable clues to the spiritual heritage of this place, which can be built upon through prayer.

I don't want to give the impression that every prayerwalker must become a historian. Prayerwalking does not require exhaustive research in order to be effective. Even if your team seems to have a talent for research, it's wise to look for ways to coordinate your efforts with other prayer leaders in your area.[5]

Develop Prayer Initiatives Based on Research

Once you've learned about the history of the area, you'll want to develop prayer initiatives based on that information. Remember that prayer leaders often are not the ones who do the research, and researchers may not be able to develop prayer initiatives. Research findings should be shared with prayer leaders who can develop a strategy for prayer, then pass it along to pastors and others who are interested in intercession.

Developing a prayer strategy may take time, and there are several steps involved. First, share information learned through research with the prayer leader. Then pray about the strategy. Seek God's mind to determine what the needs are and what prayer or prophetic acts are called for. Next, determine the membership of the team. Answer the question "Who needs to be there." Remember to communicate. A rule is to keep the city leaders or spiritual leaders informed and aware of what you are doing. Some prayer strategies are developed sequentially. For example, you might pray at first only at the perimeter of the site. On another visit, you might move deeper into the site, praying for cleansing. Finally, you might choose to perform a prophetic act that will visibly demonstrate the action you believe God will take.

Regardless of the strategy that you use, it will be informed and shaped by your historical research. How you pray for a place will be determined at least in part by the information you've gained about it.

Observe the Interplay between the Spiritual and the Natural

Even if God doesn't call you to actually do research, you can contribute to it by reporting what you see and hear. Keep a notebook in which to jot down pertinent information that you read in the newspaper, see on television, or observe on your own. Be sure to log any changes that you see in the area. George Otis Jr. notes that "having been animated by the very breath of God, we are capable of discerning spirit as well as flesh. This allows us to recognize the delicate interplay between spiritual causes and material effects and vice versa."[6] Keep your eyes open, physically and spiritually.

Identify Strongholds

By noticing the types of things cities celebrate and preserve you'll get a snapshot of what the community values. Those pictures may reveal both good and evil. In what areas does the enemy have a foothold in your community? Does that seem to be a local problem only or part of a more widespread problem? Dr. Suuqiina, the Christian Native American author of *Can You Feel the Mountains Tremble?* says, "The only ground the devil is legally entitled to is the ground given to him. He is not an heir to it, nor a steward of it in the same manner as mankind."[7]

Strongholds are wrong patterns of thought that lead to distorted behavior. That can be true of an individual or collectively of a community. For example, when something traumatic happens (such as physical abuse), the victim may develop a wrong pattern of thinking about the event, perhaps a desire for revenge. That wrong way of thinking keeps the trauma locked in and God locked out. In this way, entire communities can become strongholds of racism, injustice, or immorality. The devil is quick to capitalize on those attitudes.

What happens to us as individuals affects our whole region. When we deal with the personal strongholds we have in our lives, it gives the enemy less room to operate and allows God greater freedom to move. The same is true for our territories. God can begin to work through the prayerwalking we do.

Create a Spiritual Map

As you prayerwalk, you'll most likely be using maps already, so that you can find your way around without getting lost. A spiritual map will help direct you at another level by guiding your intercession at the places where it's needed most. Create a spiritual map by recording the places where you've prayerwalked and noting the results of your effort. If you prayerwalk consistently, it will be important to have a strategic plan, assess your results, and do follow-up. Creating a spiritual map of your area will help you to do that.[8]

Share Findings with Those Who Need Them

You only need a few people to do research, but it's important to know what to do with the information that you've gained. God can use the information to expose what He wants to remove or reveal what He wants to establish if we allow Him to direct us. Share your information with others who can sift through it to find pertinent information and pursue promising leads. You might analyze the material yourself and write a report. Others who read it may confirm your conclusions.

Occasionally, you may have information that needs to be shared with your pastor. If so, prepare a concise report that includes tentative conclusions. When you share your information with pastors or others, you must release it, avoiding the temptation to dictate what they should do with it.

God is at work in the world and in your area. When you research the spiritual history of your community, you'll get a clearer look at what God has done and at what He may now be doing. The result will be that you are better able to see God's strategy for your community and cooperate with His plan.

PRAYER ACTION LIST
How to Pray for a Historical Site

❑ Research the spiritual history of the site to determine how it may fit into God's redemptive purpose for your community.

❑ Conduct a preliminary survey, paying special attention to the commemorative purpose of the site.

❑ Coordinate with other prayer leaders to develop a strategy.

❑ Communicate your plans to church and civic leaders as necessary.

❑ Be alert for the interplay between the spiritual and the natural.

❑ Identify any strongholds that exist and determine the best prayer strategy for them.

❑ Record your findings and share the information with appropriate leaders.

PRAYER FOCUS
Historical Site

Discernment of Spirits

1 Corinthians 12:7, 8, 10: "But the manifestation of the Spirit is given to each one for the profit of all: for to one is given . . . discerning of spirits."

Father, we ask You for the discerning of spirits.

Blessing and Redeeming

Psalm 115:12–15: "The Lord has been mindful of us; He will bless us . . . He will bless those who fear the Lord, Both small and great. May the Lord give you increase more and more, You and your children. May you be blessed by the Lord. . . ."

Lord, we bless what is good.

Psalm 106:10: "He . . . redeemed them from the hand of the enemy."

We ask for God to redeem what is perverted or evil.

2 Corinthians 10:3–5(NIV): "For though we live in the world, we do not wage war as the world does. The weapons we fight with are not the weapons of the world. On the contrary, they have divine power to demolish strongholds. We demolish arguments and every pretension that sets itself up against the knowledge of God."

Father, help us to redeem this land by identifying strongholds that You want addressed.

Matthew 12:28–29: "But if I cast out demons by the Spirit of God, surely the kingdom of God has come upon you. Or how can one enter a strong man's house and plunder his goods, unless he first binds the strong man?"

We ask You to identify any strongman that is interfering with Your Spirit working in this area. Reveal the ways we are to bind the strongman.

Casting down arguments and every high thing that exalts itself against the knowledge of God, bringing every thought into captivity to the obedience of Christ.

—2 Corinthians 10:5

CHAPTER TWELVE

Calm in the Eye of the Storm

The Grossmont Union High School Board Meeting

Prayerwalk Challenge

Pray at a controversial public meeting

Prayerwalker Skill

Create prayer focus sheets

Tension had been mounting for weeks. Grossmont Union school board, anticipating an unusually large crowd, relocated its scheduled meeting to the high school gymnasium. More than 1,400 people attended.

The school board was considering adding the following words to its harassment policy: "sexual orientation, whether actual or perceived." A student board member claimed that the changes were needed because of the "extreme amount of homophobia on our campuses and the amount of discrimination towards students based on their sexual orientation," despite the fact that no incidents of harassment on campus had been recorded.[1]

Proponents of the amendment denied having ulterior motives, yet their plan was cleverly conceived. I had seen a similar strategy presented in a program on C-SPAN a few years earlier that clearly described how to handle objections to this issue from Christians. This plan was now being established in our schools—permanently. Concerned students, parents, pastors, and community members who spoke out were ignored or outright dishonored at board meetings. Board members expressed overwhelming confidence in their position and dismissed with contempt those who objected based on Judeo-Christian faith.

> My spiritual antennae had stirred while reading a newspaper article about the school district.

Three years earlier, my spiritual antennae had stirred while reading a newspaper article about the school district. "Something is going on here," I thought. I didn't feel led to pray about it so I set the matter aside.

Later, I saw another article that caused me to think. This time the feeling was stronger. It seemed as if God had written the word *Grossmont* across my chest. It felt like a small weight. "This must be on God's heart," I thought. "But what am I supposed to do with it?" Since I was new to the area, I didn't know much about the school district. I was tempted to dismiss it again. "Besides," I thought, "My children have already finished high school. Shouldn't it be parents who carry this burden?"

Yet I couldn't escape this assignment. I felt sure that I needed to pray for the Grossmont Union School District. The Grossmont administration building is located on a high school campus. I decided to take our team to prayerwalk there on Wednesday evenings. At this time, I still didn't know why God was spotlighting the schools.

Grossmont Union High School District is the second largest district in California and includes eleven high schools, 24,000 students and 2,000 staff members. It sprawls east of San Diego in the suburbs of Alpine, El Cajon, La Mesa, Lakeside, Lemon Grove, Santee, and Spring Valley. It was a strategic district for this issue, because if the questionable language could be placed in this district's policy, other districts would certainly follow its example. Although several schools in Los Angeles were on the cutting edge of this push, this would be a major decision, perhaps immobilizing Christians as a result.

In the spring of 1999 the five-member school board proposed the addition of sexual orientation language to the harassment policy. The churches were immediately alerted about the controversial proposal. Generally, area churches had not been active in civic affairs, but the pastors reluctantly alerted their congregations about the issue because of its effects on our community and our own children. Christians rallied to the issue, suspecting that the language change was a smoke screen for the promotion of the homosexual lifestyle. Proponents of the change denied that, saying that Christians were foolish for even thinking that way.

On the night of the decisive school board meeting, some of our prayer team members chose to prayerwalk discreetly outside. Several other intercessors and I felt prompted to attend the meeting. I was unsure of how well I could keep my focus on prayer during such a tense meeting, but I felt sure that I should be inside.

Representatives from more than ninety congregations came out to support righteousness. Dissenters to the proposed change expressed the view that existing policies already dealt with the issue of harassment and a new policy was not necessary. Christian leaders appealed privately with opposing board members to set up a dialog. No one was in favor of harassment; they simply wanted to present their view without being steamrollered. As I followed the alternating arguments made between two podiums, I listened for God's direction, "Pray." Then I focused on one phrase of Scripture, which I prayed silently without moving my lips. It is easier to pray more intensely from the back of an auditorium, but there are times when intercessors need to be near the front to support speakers or leaders. Using the Scriptures helped me to keep my focus. During the meeting, I used only three out of twenty Scriptures I had included on the sheet. God used the rest to prepare my heart beforehand.

> Representatives from more than ninety congregations came out to support righteousness.

In the end, however, the leading school board members rejected our voices and passed the recommendation by a 3-2 vote. That night marked a tremendous rejection of Christian values and a pivotal defeat.

In spite of that loss, our prayer team learned an important lesson—the value of prayer focus sheets. For me, the prayer focus sheet helped me to find the heart of God before attending the meeting, to become familiar with the issues by praying over them throughout the week, and to have a concise prayer agenda to follow during the meeting. I used the focus sheet to help me pray in several ways. I declared that we were complete in God and that He was the head of all principalities and powers. I periodically declared, "You are the head," enthroning God in that place. This prevented malicious or unholy anger from gaining a foothold (Col. 2:8–10). Next, I prayed for the people who had gotten together and taken counsel against our children (Ps. 83:3). I prayed also that the student and adult speakers would be able to speak with their enemies at the gate (Ps. 127:3–5).

Though we lost that battle, we eventually gained ground in the war. Within two elections, the balance of power shifted. Now four of the five board members are strong, gentle Christians. We are learning how to be citizens of Jerusalem while living in Babylon.

Using Prayer Focus Sheets

Before going to the school meeting, we prepared prayer focus sheets for our team. Using the sheets helped us to remain calm and focused on prayer during a very tense time. The idea is simple: compile a few relevant Scriptures, grouped thematically, and a few thoughts to focus your prayer, then use them both to prepare for your prayerwalk and to guide your prayers on site. Here's how you can use prayer focus sheets to make your prayerwalks more effective.

Listen for God's Voice in Worship

The purpose of a prayer focus sheet is to direct your mind toward God, so it's important to seek God's mind when compiling a sheet. Stop and spend time in worship. Open your heart to Him and allow the Holy Spirit to speak to you. You may feel directed to pray for repentance, unity, salvation for the lost, revival in the church, or any number of other issues. Seek God's heart. Let Him direct the focus of your prayers.

Identify Key Scriptures or Themes

Try to sense which Scriptures or themes God is directing you to use in prayer. One way to do this is by searching the Bible with a concordance or Bible software program. Study Bibles are helpful also, as are resources like *Vine's Complete Expository Dictionary* and *Nave's Compact Topical Bible.* Search for Scriptures that relate to the subject of your prayers. Compile a list, then sort through it to find those that God impresses upon you.

Determine a logical order for the Scriptures. For example, you might move from praise to intercession during your prayer time, so you might order the Scriptures around those sub-themes. When ordered in a logical way, the focus sheet becomes a training tool for new intercessors, teaching them an approach to prayer.

Compile the Scriptures on a Single Sheet

Print the Scriptures on a single sheet that can be easily carried and conveniently used. I like to highlight or underline words that seem especially important so I can see them easily and keep my train of thought as I walk. I also write a brief prayer or starting thought for prayer along with each Scripture. Five to eight Scriptures with prayer starters fit easily onto one side. You may have more or fewer, and you need not use all of them during your prayerwalk.

Even though we urge our team members to take the sheets home with them, I usually don't put my name or the name of any organization or church on the sheet. If it were dropped inadvertently, I wouldn't want others to think we had littered or been disrespectful in the area where we walked.

Do a Dry Run

Before you prayerwalk, ask someone to review the sheet to be sure it's easily understood. You'll want to be aware of the experience level of your team so that what you write will be useful to them. Pray through the sheet by yourself or with someone else to sense its effectiveness before using it on site.

Use Prayer Sheets to Maintain Focus

When we prayed at the school board meeting, the atmosphere was tense. The issue was a divisive one, and it would have been tempting to picture those who opposed our point of view as the enemy. Obviously, that is not the case. As Pastor Jim Garlow put it, "the purpose of government is to ensure peace, protection, and righteousness. We do not curse politicians or people who have to deal in politics in order to lead. Instead we are commanded to pray for them."[2] Using a prayer focus sheet helped me to keep my focus on the truth. I was able to pray both for God's will to be done at the meeting and for God's blessing upon those with whom I disagreed.

When you pray on site, use the prayer focus sheet to keep your prayer—and the attitude of your heart—properly directed. It is easy to become distracted by the tension of a meeting, the clamor of activity in a public place, or even the sights and sounds around you so that you fail to concentrate on the issue at hand. Build a focus into your prayer sheet, then allow that focus to direct your thoughts, your prayers, and your heart toward God as you walk and pray.

PRAYER ACTION LIST
How to Prepare a Prayer Focus Sheet

❑ Spend time in worship to seek God's mind.

❑ Sense key themes and search the Bible to identify relevant Scriptures.

❑ Determine logical order to arrange the Scriptures based on the purpose of your prayerwalk.

❑ Add a brief prayer or thought to start prayer with each Scripture.

❑ Produce a printed focus sheet in a single-page format that is easily readable.

❑ Do a dry run, asking someone else to review the content of the sheet.

❑ Use the sheet on site to help maintain your focus.

PRAYER FOCUS
Prayer Focus Sheet

Genesis 22:13–14: "Then Abraham lifted his eyes and looked, and there behind him was a ram caught in a thicket by its horns. So Abraham went and took the ram, and offered it up for a burnt offering instead of his son. And Abraham called the name of the place, The-Lord-Will-Provide [Jehovah Jireh]; as it is said to this day, "In the Mount of the Lord it shall be provided."

You, Father, are Jehhovh Jireh, our provider. You will provide the prayer focus.

Psalm 45:1 "My heart is overflowing with a good theme; I recite my compositions concerning the King; My tongue is the pen of a ready writer."

Enable the prayer focus to be written in a logical order.

Isaiah 51:16 "And I have put My words in your mouth. . . ."

Reveal the scriptures You want to put in our mouths to help us pray effectively on this assignment.

Isaiah 55:11: "So shall My word be that goes forth from My mouth; It shall not return to Me void, But it shall accomplish what I please, And it shall prosper in the thing for which I sent it."

Your word shall not return void.

Zechariah 10:12 "'So I will strengthen them in the Lord, And they shall walk up and down in His name,' Says the Lord."

We ask that the prayer focus sheet stir up prayer. Raise up more intercessors and prayerwalkers for the city.

CHAPTER THIRTEEN

Anointing the Place Where She Lay

Using Prophetic Acts

Prayerwalk Challenge

Pray on the site of a traumatic event

Prayerwalker Skill

Use prophetic acts

We arrived at the somber site where the body of seven-year-old Danielle Van Dam had been discovered in February 2002. She had been abducted and murdered. We carried with us symbols to be used in a prophetic act of cleansing. The objects we brought were intended to symbolize the salvation and healing of the grieving family, the redemption of the murderer, and the cleansing of the land that had been defiled by bloodshed, all of which we prayed would occur.

The fresh red rose carried by a fellow intercessor, symbolic of remembrance and life, seemed in sharp contrast to the dried and decaying flowers strewn about the makeshift memorial. A tender note with Scripture had been attached to the long green stem in hopes that the child's mother might find it and take comfort if she visited the place.

> My focus was on beginning the process of cleansing the land.

To the intercessor that brought the rose, the red also represented the blood of Jesus that could cleanse anyone who chose to receive it, including the man who had already been found guilty of murdering this precious child. Repentance would not protect him from the consequences of his sin—the man faced execution—yet we prayed that he would find forgiveness before he died.

Another intercessor brought a smooth stone, about palm sized, with a note attached to it, tied with a purple ribbon. Purple was chosen because it was Danielle's favorite color. Inspired by Deuteronomy 17, the stone of remembrance represented the punishment for those who break God's covenant, particularly His command, "Thou shalt not kill." The law decreed that murderers were to be stoned at the gate of the city. This stone represented justice.

My own focus was on beginning the process of cleansing the land (2 Kings 2:19–22). I had prepared by filling a small bottle with salt, a cleansing agent. I had filled another small bottle with oil, representing healing and the establishment of God's authority on that land (Ps. 23:4–5).

We stood under the shelter of a tree, gazing down at the place where the body had lain, and listening to the sounds of traffic on a distant street. The newspaper report had called this "the desert," as if it were some far away place. In fact, it was only three miles from our churches. Yes, it was barren, but many Christians traveled nearby everyday, as did gamblers on their way to a casino on the reservation.

Danielle's body was found a few feet from the golf course, on a piece of undeveloped property. The county had been scoured by hundreds of people until one volunteer, on his first day of searching, found the body. No one knows why the murderer chose that spot to leave the body. Her tiny life had been snuffed out in some other place, known only to her abductor.

When I first heard the news about Danielle's disappearance, I didn't have a hopeful feeling. I prayed that the scheme of the enemy would be exposed and that justice would be done. When the body was found twenty-seven days later, I asked God, "Why here?" And the response seemed to be, "So she could be found." The enemy had picked the wrong place to keep the crime hidden. Many intercessors in this area consistently pray that evil will be exposed. We would rather preempt evil, but when it does occur, we want it to be known.

Justice had been swift. The people from around the nation watched the televised trial, tantalized by details about the family's private life. Only seven months elapsed from the time the crime was committed until David Westerfield was found guilty. All of San Diego grieved the needless loss of a child.

Someone had fashioned a set of stairs to allow visitors to negotiate the path that led from the side of the road to Danielle's momentary resting place. While we were there, a woman stopped her car, ran up the steps carrying a new, large teddy bear, set it down, and promptly left. A young couple arrived, holding hands. They quietly looked around at the posted memorial signs. There were indications that people had prayed to other gods as well. I had visited once before but was stunned by how the site had changed. I sensed not only a spirit of grief but of chaos.

We three intercessors quoted Scripture, sang a song, then pronounced declarations as we each performed a prophetic act under God's direction, placing the rose and the stone, sprinkling salt, and pouring oil. We reverently completed our tasks for that day, believing that further instructions would surely come. God is not finished with this place.

Using Prophetic Acts

Prophetic acts are symbolic actions taken in obedience to God's leading, usually using objects found in the Bible. They symbolize the content of our prayers, declaring in a visible way the good things that we ask God to do. This simple custom is as old as Scripture—there are dozens of examples of prophetic action in the Bible, including building altars and anointing with oil. Here are some guidelines to consider when choosing to use prophetic actions in a prayerwalk.

Choose an Appropriate Action

Prayerfully select an object or an act that would symbolize most closely what would reflect God in this situation in the natural realm. When we pray, the prophetic acts God guides us to perform have great significance for blessing, reconciling, and cleansing. What is important is for us to understand their significance. Even in the Old Testament the people did not always understand completely what prophetic acts meant but were held accountable for using them anyway when God instructed them to do so. Here are a few of the things you might choose to symbolize with an action, and some of the objects or acts that would convey that meaning.

Blessing. There are a number of things that symbolize blessing. When you wish to bless homes, land, or church property, there are several things you might use. Salt and water are cleansing agents. When a place has been defiled, salt or water can be sprinkled to symbolize the spiritual cleansing of that place. There is nothing magical about either salt or water, but they can be powerful symbols of the cleansing work that God does.

Oil is another symbol of blessing. Anointing people or places with oil places a tangible symbol of God's blessing upon them. Again, there's nothing magical about the oil itself. It simply represents the richness of God and the release of faith and forgiveness (James 5:14–15). Anointing with oil represents release and restoration (Ps. 23:5; 1 Sam. 16:13).

> Anointing people or places with oil places a tangible symbol of God's blessing upon them.

Receiving communion also commemorates blessing. This reminds us of the precious atoning blood of Christ (Heb. 9:11–14).[1]

Protection. Stakes can be used as prophetic symbols of God's protection. Staking our own property as an act of faith shows that we trust God to establish protection around the property borders. Staking also declares to the enemy, "No trespassing." You might attach Scripture verses to small stakes and hammer them into the ground at the four corners of the property. These stakes might also be anointed with oil as a sign of God's blessing. Receiving communion on the land further reinforces this prophetic act. You might choose to make a proclamation like this one:

In the mighty Name of Jesus Christ, I take back every inch of land that has been controlled by the enemy. I claim this land for the kingdom of God and His righteousness. I command every demon to leave in Jesus' Name.[2]

As our prayerwalking teams have become more experienced, we have developed the habit of including some of these items in the gear that we take to prayerwalking sites. Our little kit includes salt (I prefer kosher salt), anointing oil, communion elements, and water. If we know beforehand what we might face, we ask God to show us what He would like us to do so we can be more prepared.

Dependence. Many prophetic acts are a reflection of God or our dependence on Him. Actions such as anointing with oil or blowing the shofar (a ram's horn) symbolize God's presence. In Old Testament times, a priest blew the shofar to call the people to worship or to war. We use a shofar to open many prayer services, symbolizing the voice of God. When Joshua led the people to silently march around Jericho or when singers led the nation into battle, those prophetic acts illustrated dependence on God also.

Submit to Spiritual Authority and God's Timing

Some precautions are needed when using prophetic acts. When prophetic acts involve the local church or the community at large, it's important to act under authority. As one pastor put it, "Whatever we do, let's understand spiritual government. Do not neglect to tell the pastor. Do it with some level of submission to that spiritual government."[3] There are times when you will need permission either from your church or from local authorities to perform a prophetic act. Be sure to obtain it. We do not perform prophetic acts randomly but under authority. Use discernment and get confirmation.

For prophetic acts to be effective they need to have both authority and anointing. God's perfect timing will give the act His anointing. The Holy Spirit has to lead us so we can walk in integrity.

Act Carefully

Be respectful when performing prophetic acts. Do not deface monuments or other property. And do not take God out of the prophetic act and just follow a procedure. Remember, it is the power of the prayer behind the prophetic act that counts, not the action itself.

Also, beware of publicizing prophetic acts. If Christians publicize prophetic acts inappropriately, occult groups may take the opportunity to perform spiritual actions of their own. Be aware that those involved in the occult understand the dark side of the spiritual world. They aim to tap into demonic power. We are not fearful of them, just wise and cautious. When you are in doubt about whether or not to perform some prophetic act, ask the leader of your group or your pastor.

Other Christians may occasionally question the value of a prophetic act that you believe God has directed you to perform. When that happens, proceed with confidence but not defiance.

Be careful not to ritualize these acts or put faith in them. Rather, our focus should always be on the Lord, who sometimes leads us to prophetic action.

Jesus brings us into a Covenant with God. Because of this Covenant, we don't pray for ourselves only but also for future generations who will inhabit the places where we prayerwalk and, we pray, will enter the Covenant through faith in Christ.

In Joshua 4, God told Joshua to pile up twelve stones as a reminder of His faithfulness to Israel in leading them through the Jordan River and into the Promised Land. These stones were intended to leave a permanent marker for future generations. "This pile of stones will be a reminder for you," Joshua said to the people, "When our children ask in later years, 'What are these stones here for? Why are they piled up like this?' then we will have an answer for them" (Josh. 4:6–7, author's paraphrase). Pastor Jim Garlow finishes the story this way:

> In verses 21–24 of the same chapter, after they had put the stones in place, Joshua reminded them again, "When your children ask their fathers in time to come, saying, 'What are these stones?' then you shall inform your children, saying, 'Israel crossed this Jordan on dry ground.' For the LORD your God dried up the waters of the Jordan before you until you had crossed, just as the LORD your God had done to the Red Sea, which He dried up before us until we had crossed; that all the peoples of the earth may know that the hand of the LORD is mighty, so that you may fear the LORD your God forever."

What a thrill it must have been when many of the younger ones who had crossed the Jordan came back in their later years with their children and grandchildren and heard their grandchildren ask, "Grandpa, why are these stones here?" With a smile they would tell the story of God's faithfulness many years before. This was a reminder of a covenant that God had not only made but also kept. And He had kept it for the future generations as well.[4]

The role you play today affects the generations to come. As those who come behind us find evidence of our faithful prayers, they will be encouraged in their faith.

PRAYER ACTION LIST
How to Use Prophetic Acts

❑ Choose an action that you feel reflects God's will for the situation.

❑ Submit to spiritual authority and civil authorities, including receiving permission when necessary.

❑ Aim to sense God's timing for the prophetic act.

❑ Make a Scripture-based declaration, proclaiming the purpose of the prophetic action.

❑ Act with respect to those around you and do not call attention to yourself unnecessarily.

❑ Use the prophetic action to commemorate your faith and to pray for the faith of others.

PRAYER FOCUS
Walking As a Prophetic Act

Joshua 1:3: "Every place that the sole of your foot will tread upon I have given you. . . ."

Father, we anoint our feet with oil as a symbol of establishing Your authority because You give us authority where you call us to walk.

Luke 10:19: "Behold, I give you the authority to trample on serpents and scorpions, and over all the power of the enemy. . . ."

Lord, You give authority to trample over the power of the enemy.

Joshua 10:24–25: "So it was, when they brought out those kings to Joshua, that Joshua called for all the men of Israel, and said to the captains of the men of war who went with him, 'Come near, put your feet on the necks of these kings.' And they drew near and put their feet on their necks. Then Joshua said to them, 'Do not be afraid, nor be dismayed; be strong and of good courage, for thus the Lord will do to all your enemies against whom you fight.'"

Father, when there is a war in our life or a situation, we symbolically put our foot on the neck of our enemy. As a prophetic act, we walk, dance, march and stomp on the enemy.

Deuteronomy 33:29c: "Your enemies shall submit (cower) to you, And you shall tread down their high places."

Cause us to tread upon the high places of Your enemies.

Job 40:12 (NASB): "Look on everyone who is proud, and humble him; And tread down the wicked where they stand."

We tread on the proud enemy that is working in or through this situation. We call down pride in Jesus name.

Ezekiel 6:11 (NASB) "Thus says the Lord God: 'Clap your hand, stamp your foot, and say. . .'"

Father, we clap our hands and stomp our feet and make a proclamation that "Every place on which the sole of our foot treads shall be Yours. No man shall be able to stand against You" (Deut. 11:20–25).

Afterword

I n this book I have shared some of what have come to be my reminder stones. These stones line the path that I walk as I take the name of Jesus with me. The way has not always been smooth or easy or comfortable, but it has been a good journey because I have grown in my faith and in my practice of prayer. I've become more aware of the spiritual warfare that takes place around us every day, but I'm not afraid of the battle. Christ has already won the victory.

I know that the enemy will try to dissuade you from prayerwalking. He'll present a million reasons why you can't, or shouldn't, do this, just as he did to me. But don't be discouraged. Remember that "He who is in you is greater than he who is in the world" (1 John 4:4). With each spiritual victory, you will be encouraged to keep walking on.

I pray that as you embark on the journey of prayer, you, too, may find reminder stones, and that your faith and joy in the Lord may be greater with each step. May the blessing of Deut. 11:22–25 be upon you as you take the name of Jesus with you wherever you go.

> For if you carefully keep all these commandments which I command you to do—to love the LORD your God, to walk in all His ways, and to hold fast to Him—then the LORD will drive out all these nations from before you, and you will dispossess greater and mightier nations than yourselves. Every place on which the sole of your foot treads shall be yours. . . . No man shall be able to stand against you; the LORD your God will put the dread of you and the fear of you upon all the land where you tread, just as He has said to you.

Notes

Introduction: Jehovah Shammah

1. Steve Hawthorne and Graham Kendrick, *Prayerwalking: Praying On Site with Insight* (Orlando, Fla.: Creation House, 1993), 16.

2. Ted Haggard, *Taking It to the Streets—How Dynamic Prayerwalking Changes Lives and Transforms Cities* (Colorado Springs, Colo.: Wagner Publications, 2002), 8–11.

3. I am indebted for this paradigm of authority to Arthur Burk's tape series *Earning Authority over Freemasonry*, tape 1, "Coming in the Opposite Spirit," (Whittier, Calif.: Plumbline Ministries).

4. Ibid.

Chapter 1: Prayer Letters to the Editor

1. Barbara Wentroble, *Prophetic Intercession*, (Ventura, Calif.: Renew, 1999), 57–58.

2. Chuck D. Pierce and Rebecca Wagner Sytsema, *The Best Is Yet Ahead* (Colorado Springs, Colo.: Wagner Publications, 2001), 18.

3. Cindy Jacobs, *The Voice of God* (Ventura, Calif.: Regal Books, 1995), 79.

Chapter 2: The Day God Fixed the Media Truck

1. Cindy Tosto, *Taking Possession of the Land: A Step-by-Step Guide to Transforming Your Neighborhood Through Strategic Prayer* (Colorado Springs, Colo.: Wagner Publications, 2001), 50–51.

2. Cindy Jacobs describes this concept beautifully as "The Clean Heart Principle" in her book *Possessing the Gates of the Enemy* (Grand Rapids, Mich.: Chosen Books, 1994), 40.

Chapter 3: Lemon Grove 91945

1. Dutch Sheets, *Beginner's Guide to Intercession* (Ann Arbor, Mich.: Vine Books, 2001), 30.

2. Steve Hawthorne, *Prompts for Prayerwalkers* (Austin, Tex.: WayMakers), 14.

Chapter 4: Hidden in Plain View

1. I highly recommend Carolyn Sundeth's book about her prayer-walking experiences, *Barefoot to the White House* (Altamonte Springs, Fla.: Creation House, 1992).

2. Arthur Salm, "Center receives cleansing, GOP spirit exorcised," *San Diego Union-Tribune*, 19 August 1996.

3. Cindy Jacobs, *Possessing the Gates of the Enemy: A Training Manual for Militant Intercession* (Grand Rapids, Mich.: Chosen Books, 1994), 59.

Chapter 5: The Sisters I Never Knew

1. Martha Featherston, Interfaith Prayer Fellowship, 5767 Hughes Street, San Diego, CA 92115. Mamie Leonard Ministries, P.O. Box 431755, Los Angeles, CA 90043.

2. Richard Twiss, *One Church Many Tribes: Following Jesus the Way God Made You*, (Ventura, Calif.: Regal Books, 2000), 23. Richard is president of Wiconi International, www.wiconi.com.

3. Mary Hutchinson, "Native American Believers Gather to Forgive 'White Man' of Injustices," *Charisma* (December 2002): 18.

4. For more on this subject see John Dawson, *Healing America's Wounds* (Ventura, Calif.: Regal Books, 1994), 24, and George Otis Jr, *Informed Intercession* (Ventura, Calif.: Renew, 1999), 254.

5. Gwen Sherrer, *Good Night Lord* (Ventura, Calif.: Regal Books, 2000), 147.

Chapter 6: The Church That Bought a Fire Truck

1. Conversation with Officer Mequel Penulosa, San Diego Poice Department, San Diego, Calif., 17 December 2002.

Chapter 7: Announcing God's Plans on Television

1. Chuck Pierce and Rebecca Wagner Sytsema, *The Future War of the Church* (Ventura, Calif.: Renew, 2001), 147.

Chapter 8: The Power of Joining Hands

1. Bonnie H. Shannonhouse, Tapestry, P.O. Box 1621, Annapolis, Md., 21404, www.TapestryLostCoin.org.

2. Cindy Jacobs, *Possessing the Gates of the Enemy: A Training Manual for Militant Intercession* (Grand Rapids, Mich.: Chosen Books, 1994), 93.

3. Terry Teykl, *Preyed on or Prayed For*, (Muncie, Ind.: Prayer Point Press, 2000), 125.

4. Jacobs, *Possessing the Gates*, 95.

5. Edgardo Silvoso, *That None Should Perish* (Ventura, Calif.: Regal Books, 1994), 155.

6. Ted Haggard, *Primary Purpose* (Orlando, Fla.: Creation House, 1995), 88.

7. Teykl, *Preyed on or Prayed For*, 94.

Chapter 9: Marching in the Shadow of Man

1. C. Peter Wagner, *Engaging the Enemy* (Ventura, Calif.: Regal Books, 1999), 160.

Chapter 10: When God Came Back to the Mountain

1. Chuck D. Pierce and Rebecca Wagner Sytsema, *The Future War of the Church* (Ventura, Calif.: Renew Books, 2001), 86.

Chapter 11: We Walked for Three Hundred Years in One Day

1. Steve Hawthorne made a video tape of this project called *"The California Prayer Walk: San Diego to San Francisco, March 1–April 9, 1995."* Copies are available from Waymakers, 512.331.8205.

2. Raymond G. Starr, *San Diego: A Pictorial History* (Norfolk, Va.: The Donning Company Publishers, 1986), 53.

3. George Otis, Jr., *Informed Intercession*, (Ventura, Calif.: Renew Books, 1999), 254.

4. Ibid., 130. Other helpful resources for researching the spiritual history of an area are *Releasing Heaven on Earth* by Alistair Petrie, and *Can You Feel the Mountains Tremble? A Healing the Land Handbook* by Dr. Suuqiina. Suuqiina's book is the simplest and most concise. Petrie gives a biblical understanding of the stewardship of land and how people, churches, communities, and cities are affected by it. He explains how to identify the spiritual forces that hinder effective evangelism.

5. Two possibilities are the Sentinel Group and the World Prayer Center, though there are other organizations that serve as information clearinghouses. George Otis Jr. heads the Sentinel Group (www.sentinelgroup.org or 800.668.5657). The World Prayer Center in

Colorado Springs, Colo., partners with Global Harvest Ministry, which tracks spiritual mapping projects (www.globalharvestministries.org or 719.262.9922).

6. George Otis, Jr., *Informed Intercession*, 130.

7. Dr. Suuqiina, *Can You Feel the Mountains Tremble? A Healing the Land Handbook* (Anchorage, Alaska: Inuit Ministries International, 1999), 16.

8. A helpful resource for spiritual mapping is *The Redemptive Gifts of Cities,* an eight tape series by Arthur Burk, available from Plumbline Ministries (plumblineministries.com).

Chapter 12: Calm in the Eye of the Storm

1. Allyson Smith, "Gay Steamroller" *San Diego News Notes*, July/August 1999.

2. Message by Pastor Jim Garlow, "Living Christian-ly in This World," Skyline Wesleyan Church, La Mesa, Calif., November 2–3, 2002.

Chapter 13: Anointing the Place Where She Lay

1. For more on the value of these symbols of blessing, see Alistair Petrie, *Releasing Heaven On Earth* (Grand Rapids, Mich.: Chosen Books, 2000), 190–200.

2. For more on this type of action, see Henry Malone, *Portals to Cleansing* (Irving, Tex.: Vision Life Publications, 2002), 4.

3. Conversation with Pastor Gary Goodell, Meta Church, San Diego, Calif., 15 March 2003.

4. James L. Garlow, *The Covenant* (Kansas City, Mo.: Beacon Hill Press of Kansas City, 1999), 58–59.